SCORE!

POWER UP YOUR
GAME | BUSINESS | LIFE
BY HARNESSING THE POWER OF EMOTIONAL INTELLIGENCE

JOHN BOTHWELL
DAVID GEIER

MORGAN JAMES PUBLISHING · NEW YORK

SCORE!

POWER UP YOUR
GAME | BUSINESS | LIFE
BY HARNESSING THE POWER OF EMOTIONAL INTELLIGENCE

John Bothwell & David Geier

Copyright ©2006 John Bothwell & David Geier

ISBN: 1-933596-62-7 (Hardcover)
ISBN: 1-60037-006-3 (Paperback)
ISBN: 1-60037-007-1 (eBook)

Published by:

MORGAN · JAMES
THE ENTREPRENEURIAL PUBLISHER ™
www.morganjamespublishing.com

Morgan James Publishing, LLC
1225 Franklin Ave Ste 32
Garden City, NY 11530-1693
Toll Free 800-485-4943
www.MorganJamesPublishing.com

Cover/Interior Design by:
Rachel Campbell
rcampbell77@cox.net

Habitat
for Humanity®
Peninsula
Building Partner

DEDICATIONS | This book is dedicated to five miracles in my life: My wife Renee the love of my life, and our three children, my daughters, Nicole, and Virginia, and my son John.

Last but certainly not least to my grandfather Walter Corlett, who demonstrated unconditional love, and has been a life long friend and mentor. Thank you all.

John Bothwell

To Mary, Jon, and Jackie.
"Each new day is an opportunity to live a life full of joy and gladness."
David Geier

WHAT OTHERS HAVE TO SAY | I am a

partner in a successful business coaching organization as well as a golfer. I can say that after reading the book I personally have gained further insight into evaluating my personal life as well as business and the game of golf. The emotional intelligence concepts taught in the book have wide application to all of life's challanges and I would reccommend it to anyone who is looking to improve themselves at any level.

JACK MENCINI
Maximum Value Partners, LLC
www.maximumvp.com

Score! Power up your Game/Business/and Life, Harnessing the Power of Emotional Intelligence is a breakthrough book giving the reader a clear understanding on how to learn and apply the skill sets of emotional intelligence. No matter if you are a CEO, manager, parent, spouse, or athlete, raising your emotional intelligence, by following David and John's EQ principles, can only help you to become more highly successful in all walks of life.

BOB KOCH, President
Medicus Golf

Unlike IQ, EQ (Emotional Intelligence) is something humans develop throughout their lives. Bothwell & Geier give a fabulous explanation of EQ and the role it plays in our game, business and life. Reading SCORE! will help you react positively to difficult situations on the golf course and in your life. It will also assist you at becoming a better partner.

BERNIE BEAUDOIN
Sales & Marketing

TABLE OF CONTENTS |

FOREWORD | *Score! Power Up Your Game, Business and Life By Harnessing the Power of Emotional Intelligence* is **AN INTRODUC-TORY BOOK ON EMOTIONAL INTELLIGENCE.** Emotional Intelligence is often called EQ or EI. The "EQ" acronym has the advantage of suggesting a parallel with "IQ", the well-known measure of effective thinking and problem solving. EQ is a measure of emotional effectiveness that deals with feelings and motivational states.

IN THIS BOOK, WE INTRODUCE THE READER TO THE KEY CONCEPTS THAT UNDERLIE EMOTIONAL INTELLIGENCE AS THEY RELATE TO THE WORLDS OF BUSINESS AND GOLF. In addition, we introduce two sample emotional intelligence assessments, one for business and one for golf. Taken together, the businessperson/golfer will have a much clearer understanding of the emotional skills which will help him or her to become more successful in either the workplace or on the golf course.

TODAY, WE HAVE FEW PRACTICAL ROAD MAPS OR BLUE-PRINTS FOR SHOWING CHILDREN, YOUNG ADULTS AND ADULTS HOW TO BECOME MORE HIGHLY DEVELOPED AND MATURE. In the education and business worlds, the hard skills for learning task-oriented skills, still reign supreme. Soft skills, which teach emotional, mental, transpersonal and spiritual skills, are being overshadowed in the schools and in many churches today. Yet, the current research on emotional intelligence suggests that soft skills may, in fact, be 12 times more important than hard skills. As Daniel Goleman, an expert in the field of emotional intelligence, has stated, hard skills (the task oriented skills) help us to get a job, while the soft skills (the personal and social people skills) are what get us promoted.

WE CHOSE THE TITLE, *Score! Power Up Your Game, Business and Life By Harnessing the Power of Emotional Intelligence*, because business and golf do go together. According to the National Golf Foundation, nearly 98% of the CEOs of Fortune 500 companies play golf as their sport of choice. Secondly, we believe that most long-term development occurs when it can be practiced as an on-going activity, much like practicing a musical instrument, yoga, a martial art or any athletic discipline. By teaching the emotional intelligence skills through a popular sport, such as golf, the emotional intelligence skills-sets can be more readily transferred into the work and home environments, thereby increasing the probabilities of success.

IN THE FINAL ANALYSIS, THIS BOOK IS A GUIDE AND A ROAD MAP TO INTRODUCE TEENAGERS, YOUNG ADULTS AND ADULTS TO THE EMOTIONAL INTELLIGENCE CONCEPTS AND PRINCIPLES THAT CAN LEAD THEM TO BECOME MORE MATURE AND BALANCED AS HUMAN BEINGS. We encourage each reader to seriously reflect on each topic presented and apply them, one by one, to their consciousness and daily activities. The benefits will certainly help each reader to grow and have a profound impact on our society and the global community.

JOHN BOTHWELL, PH.D. AND DAVID GEIER

HOW DID WE BECOME WHO WE ARE?

INTRODUCTION | Nicole was one year old.

To celebrate, we invited her loving aunts and uncles, four doting grandparents and many close friends, all of whom spent several hours decorating the home with 'Happy Birthday' banners, colorful balloons and streamers, and it was clear to all that Nicole enjoyed being the center of attention. I've observed that, later in her life, she still enjoys being the center of attention, which may have more to do with being first born than her first birthday party.

When her mom brought out the chocolate birthday cake, the celebrants broke into an off-key rendition of "Happy Birthday to You" as Mom and Dad helped Nicole blow out the single candle on the cake to loud applause. Nicole was absolutely delighted and applauded along with her guests. But then the fun really began.

The cake was placed on Nicole's high chair tray while friends and relatives watched expectantly. She was a bit confused, looked at the guests, at the cake, at the guests - before grabbing a fistful of frosting and cramming it into her mouth.

The crowd howled with laughter, cameras flashed and Nicole beamed from ear to ear, grabbing handfuls of cake and eating every bite she could.

Indeed, all - especially one-year-old Nicole - had a fun time, and the pictures of that special day 33 years ago prove it. Today, Nicole is a business owner and highly successful legal marketing consultant - a long way from her face-first nosedive into that chocolate cake.

The point of the story? As an infant, Nicole acted as expected. The day was all about her. She reveled in the moment and, when presented with a tasty, three-layer chocolate birthday cake, well, she did what any one-year old would do. She dove in without a second thought, smeared cake as far as her little arms could reach and smiled broadly at the cheers and laughter of loved ones.

Today, if Nicole were put into the same circumstances - relatives, decorations, and a three-layer cake - it would be highly unlikely that she would grab fistfuls of cake to smear from ear to ear. Instead, the cake would be cut, appropriately sized pieces served and the guests—and Nicole—would talk about family, friends and her son's up-coming first birthday party.

What had changed? Obviously, Nicole grew up. She has been educated, socialized, indoctrinated; she's been tested, inspected, analyzed and evaluated. Assessment metrics were devised, her profile was on file, and Nicole had become a walking, talking contributor to society.

So, no biggie, right? Some kid grew up. Big deal, so did you, so did I, so do we all. No, it's no biggie. But the steps that Nicole went through from her first birthday to today have been complex, sometimes difficult and, in two words: downright amazing!

At the age of one, Nicole acted as any one-year old would when presented with a giant cake covered with sweet, chocolate frosting—she went to work. There was no regard for manners, no regard for the mess, no regard for the other guests (most of whom passed on a clump of baby-mashed b-day cake) - in fact, as far as young Nicole was concerned all those years ago, she was the center of the universe and she could eat cake with her hands if she wanted to.

If she acted like that today, in all likelihood she wouldn't receive many invitations to parties - especially birthday parties!

From the time little Nicole was one-year old, to the time she reached her 33rd birthday, she experienced a number of developmental stages. As any parent knows, these stages occur on a fairly set timetable.

Nicole, just like other children, went through a normal gestation period of about nine months. At eight months, she began to develop a number of emotions to let mommy and daddy know how she was feeling. (You should have heard her at age two.)

By age three, Nicole had reached a low-level mental stage and was beginning to think in terms of concrete concepts, perceptions and images. In addition, Nicole was developing an egocentric personality. She had developed the ability to let us know which of her toys were not to be touched. And, at this stage of development, Nicole actually did believe in The Velveteen Rabbit, monsters under the bed, and Santa Claus.

By the age of seven, Nicole began to take on another role. She was starting to become less egocentric (self-centered) and more ego-empathic, with some parental guidance and, of course, the experience of attending school with peers. By ages eight and nine, Nicole was becoming a socialized citizen of her community. She also learned to follow the rules and to be a decent human being, from her parents, teachers, and other authority figures. And, she was learning how to give back something to her community through her participation in the Brownies and our local church community.

By ten or eleven, the pre-adolescent Nicole had reached a more advanced mental stage wherein she could manipulate abstract concepts and thoughts and visualize consequences to her actions and words.

And by age eighteen, Nicole was fully able to think about deeper questions like, "I think, therefore, I am" and "Who am I?" Nicole was well on her way to becoming a fully mature human being. She had matured, and her development was more integrated. Yes —Nicole was on the verge of even higher and deeper development

PERSONAL DEVELOPMENT IN GOLF. In golf, player development, just like human development, occurs in a series of stages. These stages are generally described as:

- Technical/Physical – learning swing mechanics, being in good physical condition.
- Emotional – getting frustrated, angry, and impatient when not performing well or feeling joyful, happy, and peaceful.
- Mental – visualizing and planning a shot, creating goals for performance.
- Transpersonal – become a third party witness/observer rather than an critical judger of each golf shot, being aware within the present moment and personally motivated by the energies that internally drives the individual. Playing golf with a vision and purpose will improve enjoyment.
- Spiritual – golf becomes a vehicle for personal transformation by practicing meditation, helping others to grow through mentoring, providing service to others, being kind and compassionate to all living things.

In addition, golfers and humans grow along a variety of developmental lines. This means that people grow in more than one way. What's even more interesting is the fact that development is far from being an even or balanced process.

A business owner may have well-developed cognitive abilities (knowledge applications, analysis, evaluation) and moral development (right and wrong, values), but may be under-developed in interpersonal skills (social relationships), and even low in psychological needs development (personal security and a sense of belonging).

In golf, a player may rate high in the short game, but average in driving the ball 250 yards with accuracy, and low in reading a putt or controlling his or her emotions after hitting a shot out of bounds.

To bring the developmental lines into balance, a person first needs to create a baseline to measure personal strengths and under-developed skills. Then, a well-rounded training strategy can be designed with specific practices to allow the capacities and attributes to develop over time.

Today, learning emotional intelligence skills in golf is essential, because as most players know, golf is not simply a physical game. It's just as much an emotional and mental game. And from what we know about emotional intelligence, EQ has the ability to produce better results, from bottom line profitability in business to lower scores on the course.

———◆———

THE HUMAN: A SOCIAL ANIMAL. Ever since our ancestors were running from mastodons and squatting in caves, humans have been a sociable group. Now that doesn't mean that we like to party hearty (though who doesn't, now and then); it simply means that humans like to be around other humans.

Think about your own life. From where do you derive the most pleasure and the most satisfaction? From your relationships with family and friends, co-workers and neighbors, teammates, lodge brothers and all of the relationships you have with other humans. Without the other humans with whom we interact daily, life simply wouldn't be as much fun.

To live social lives - to be members of a society - requires that we all become self-aware and socialized. In other words, we learn the rules of acceptable behavior within our society.

And, of course, those rules will change from one society to another. For example, in some remote societies, the eldest member of the tribe always eats the boar's eyes - a real delicacy. In contemporary Western societies, whoever calls 'dibs' gets the boar's eyes for dessert.

The process of socialization takes many years because there's so much information to learn:

1 | We have to learn the language and the lingo - not only the words themselves but also the variety of meanings behind the words. Word context, tone of voice, facial expression - all of these aspects of effective communication must be learned as a part of the process of socialization.

2 | We have to learn the social conventions of our society. We learn good manners, we learn to be polite and how to behave around others.

3 | We must learn the traditions and history of our society - how we got to where we are today. In some societies, that means learning about the day the sun god fought with the moon god. In other societies, it's learning about holidays, important dates and the triumphs and tragedies of the social group. Be it a small tribe or a modern, industrial nation, the process is much the same.

4 | We must learn the laws of our societies - the taboos and the tax laws, tribal justice or judicial tribunal. Laws direct our actions and provide the guidelines for acceptable behavior.

5 | We must accept the social contract by which we are all bound. As productive, law abiding members of any society; we must agree to live by the rules and laws of the society. In return for doing our part, we get to live within the society. If we fail to live up to our end of the social contract, we're forced to leave the society. That can mean banishment to the next ice floe that passes by, or 25 to life in a maximum-security prison. (Obviously, it pays to keep up your end of the deal.)

6 | Then there are the society's institutions - religions, government, schools and learning centers, recreation, family structure and family life - the list just goes on and on. And as with all of these aspects of socializing children, the newest members of the society, the institutions will change from one society to another. In the US, baseball is a revered institution. Deep in the Brazilian rain forest, a different society, baseball is unknown.

WHY SOCIALIZE? Simply put: because if we didn't socialize children as they grow, the structure of society would collapse and we would be back living in mud huts fighting with the folks in the next valley over who's better, the god of the trees or the god of the shrubberies.

The socializing process is essential for the maintenance of the society and for moving the society forward. Without it, the accumulated knowledge of the society would be lost. Each generation would have to relearn which plants cured which illnesses, or in the case of our modern, industrial societies, how to use the TV remote. Socialization enables a society - big, small or somewhere in between - to remain cohesive and to grow. Think about it. If we didn't pass on the discoveries and knowledge of those who came before us, technology would simply cease to exist (which may be viewed as either a good or bad thing by different people in different societies).

This Morning's Headlines. Make a quick scan of this morning's paper. Doesn't matter which day, any day will do. As you skim the headlines, you'll find at least one story that will make you scratch your head and mutter something about, "...the world going to hell in a hand basket."

A husband kills his wife, the mother of his children. A drifter abducts a young child and kills her. Riots here. Cruelty there. You don't have to look too far to find instances of individuals who, for one reason or another, failed the socialization and emotional intelligence test.

You may wonder how such a thing is possible. What would drive someone to take the life of another with callousness and without remorse? What would cause a nation's leader to order the killing of tens of thousands of people while he's vacationing on the Mediterranean? From the smallest act of cruelty to mass genocide, it's obvious that not everyone is willing to accept socialization, nor are they aware, both internally and externally, of the effects of their actions. In many cases, these people rewrite their own conventions and limits of what's acceptable and what isn't.

The world is far from a perfect place because we are far from a perfect species. We have base emotions - anger, jealousy, resentment and greed. We hate because our ancestors hated. We act without reason, without a thought to the consequences of our actions. We kill for sport, we break the laws and taboos, and we ignore our obligation to adhere to the social contract. And the results are the stuff that fills our history books and the morning paper

- from the Holocaust (unfathomable) to the spousal abuser who lives down the block (also unfathomable).

EQ ON THE COURSE; EQ ON THE JOB

The world of business and the game of golf share many common characteristics. Both require anticipation, planning, the development of skills. Both have a final goal - business success or the best score you've ever shot. Both require a mixture of power and finesse, strength and control.

The parallels between the games of business and golf are numerous, and so is the connection between business, golf, and emotional intelligence (your EQ), as you'll soon discover. The management of emotions, whether delivering a talk to shareholders or delivering the ball from the trap to the green, is essential to success.

THE EGO AT TWO YEARS OF AGE. We all know how our kids are. They run up and down the aisles at restaurants as we chase after them. They wake up in the middle of the night crying because they want something. The words "me," "my," and "I" are the most overused words in their developing vocabularies. That's because a child under the age of three years is the center of the universe - at least as far as he or she is concerned.

The concept of 'others' in the child's world is limited. Others are there to tend to the child's needs. And when those needs aren't met, well, we've all seen the red-faced child mid-tantrum in the candy aisle at the local supermarket. To these youngsters, the word 'no' isn't informational - it's confrontational.

> Child: Daddy, can I have dat? (points to candy bar)
> Daddy: No. (confrontational)
> Child: But I want it. (the ego speaks)
> Daddy: No. It'll ruin your appetite. (an appeal to reason)
> Child: Noooo. I want it. I waaannnttt it! (the ego wails)
> Daddy: I said 'no'. Now please be quiet. (an appeal to socialize)

Then, with lip quivering and eyes welling with tears, the child breaks into a chorus of "I want it. I want it. I want it now. Nooow!" as the father looks sheepishly at the other customers waiting in the checkout lines.

The ego of a child is the driving force in their thoughts and deeds. There is no consideration of the consequences, no analysis of the particular situation, no thought for others. The child simply knows what they want and when she wants it, which is usually - now!

Now does this indicate that there's something wrong with children? Of course, not. Children act like...well, children. They have little control over their wants and needs. Rather their activities are driven by their wants and needs. The simple fact is, children are just beginning to develop emotional intelligence, or EQ. They haven't gone through the process of socialization & self-awareness. They haven't learned to consider the feelings of others. Kids will say whatever pops into their heads, often to our chagrin. ("Mommy, what's wrong with that man!")

Studies have shown that children under the age of three lack the language skills, the reasoning skills and the desire to develop emotional intelligence, and while the concept of emotional intelligence is easy to understand, it's a difficult concept to master - even for adults...even for adults with very high IQs (intelligence quotients). So, we shouldn't expect much from young kids. Having said that, your child's early EQ development may very well be a product of his or her environment (nurturing vs. non-supportive).

However, EQ is something that we all learn as part of the socialization process. Over time, as we gather life experience, we learn that the universe does not revolve around us and that we must control and harness our emotions. In other words, we must integrate our egos into the larger whole, the complete individuals that we become.

And it doesn't take much to look around to see that some people have done a better job of integrating their own egos than others. For example, those with developed EQs are able to put the needs of others before their own when appropriate. They can empathize with others. Those who consistently put their own needs first, still have a way to go toward integrating their egos into the total self - the total human being they'll become.

HOW TO PLAY NICE WITH OTHERS. First, there's you. An individual like no other. A collection of experiences, knowledge, emotions, desires and needs. This is the internal you - the you that thinks to himself, the you who has secrets, the you who is kept partially hidden from the rest of the world, and the you that only you know completely - strengths and weaknesses. This is the ego-driven you - the you who wants a better car, a bigger house, a better job, a lower golf score. (But I want it!)

But you don't exist alone. Like the rest of humankind, you are a social animal. You belong to many different groups. You're the member of a family. A team. A community. You're a citizen, a co-worker, a spouse, a brother or sister, mother or father, a Republican or a Democrat, an 'us' or a 'them'.

These are your interpersonal relationships with other human beings. And it's within these various relationships that emotional intelligence plays a critical role. Think about the people you know, your friends and family, the people at the office, your manager, the guy who mows your lawn, or the woman who cut you off on the way to work this morning.

Some of these people are kind, generous, giving and forgiving. They express love and disappointment with the same intensity and with the same care. They work and play well with others, whether on the playground at recess, throughout the workday or while practicing at the local range facility. In all situations, these people have integrated their egos into a unified whole - a complete individual who plays (and works) well with others.

The signs of emotional intelligence revel themselves in many ways. Are you willing to accept criticism graciously? Do you cooperate with co-workers, with your neighbors and your spouse? Are you willing to put the needs of others - even complete strangers - ahead of your own needs when appropriate? Some of us are. Many of us are not. That's what this book is all about - your EQ, and how to develop it in the workplace, on the golf course (where the ability to control or manage your emotions is critical) and in virtually every other aspect of your life. The objective is to make you a happier, healthier, well-adjusted social animal (human being)—something for which we all strive.

Learning to play and work with others is something we learn as children. Some people are adept at social interaction. Others never learn to see beyond themselves, their wants and needs.

Into which group do you fall?

THE 2-YEAR-OLD EGO IN A 32-YEAR-OLD BODY

Sadly, not all people develop the emotional intelligence needed to get along with others. The whack-job driver who tailgates inches off your bumper, the rude woman who cuts in line at the theater, the noisy diners sitting next to you in a posh eatery - these are all examples of the two-year old ego living in an adult's body.

These are the people who put themselves first. These are the people who are oblivious to the feelings of others and oblivious to how others see them. You might call them selfish, self-absorbed or egocentric.

The point: just because you grow physically, just because you acquire knowledge and develop intellectual skills, does not mean that you will develop EQ as a matter of course. In fact, most people never realize the full potential of their EQ.

You know them. You see them as they move blithely through their lives, apparently unconscious of others around them. They are bullies in the work place. They are rude to the staff. They yell (an adult-sized tantrum) when things don't go their way. You interact with them throughout each day. And, maybe you are one of these people who never had the opportunity to develop your EQ.

———————◆———————

MANAGING EMOTIONS IN GOLF TO RAISE PERFORMANCE.

Many of the top pros in golf have trained and learned to manage their emotions in life and on the course. This includes managing both their positive and negative emotions. They're able to do this by minimizing the length of time they will attach themselves to the emotional states they are experiencing. In addition, they can control the types of thoughts they are creating for planning a shot as well as keeping their minds quiet during the execution of the golf shot.

But keep in mind that even someone as developed as Tiger Woods gets angry after hitting a below average shot, or highly excited after making a great chip shot. This is part of Tiger's behavioral nature. He gets angry when he hits poor shots that he knows he's capable of executing; and he can get very pumped up when he makes a miraculous shot. However, holding onto the emotions of either result can be unproductive.

The difference though, is that players like Tiger Woods, Annika Sorenstam, Ernie Els, and Carrie Webb can usually place a time limit on how long they'll remain in an emotional state. The amateur golfer, however, may hold onto their negative emotional states for a much longer period of time, causing them to play with less consistency.

The work that professional golfers do with their sports psychologists, helps them develop a capacity to become more self aware of their emotional states. This, in turn, teaches the professional to recognize their emotions while they are experiencing them. Then, as a result of their training, they can quickly return to an emotional state that is more calm, directed and competitive.

It is this ability to recognize one's emotional states while they are happening and understand their effects (called self-awareness), that separates a person with lower versus higher levels of emotional intelligence. By managing one's emotional states as they arise, golfers can increase their chances of shooting lower scores on a consistent basis.

WHERE DO YOU BEGIN? The answer to where do you begin will be found in chapters two and three. These chapters will provide you with information on how to assess where you stand today, and secondly, to help you grow your emotional intelligence in the workplace, and in the great game we can play for a lifetime – golf.

In addition, we will provide you with many thought-provoking questions and practical exercises in emotional intelligence. The more you consciously think about the questions and practice them in business, golf, parenting, and marriage; the more you will be able to raise your emotional intelligence over time.

So, read on. Discover that it's never too late to become a more complete human being. It's never too late to develop empathy and compassion. It's never too late to learn to play well with others. The good news is, Emotional Intelligence can be learned regardless of your age or your IQ.

Learning the emotional intelligence skills of self- awareness, self-confidence, self-control and adaptability is not simply for top tour professionals or top executives. On the contrary, amateur golfers today, especially those playing business golf or in amateur tournaments, need to learn how to raise their emotional intelligence if they want to play at their best - and who doesn't want to play at their best?

A Brief History of Emotional Intelligence

CHAPTER ONE | For millennia, human emotions have played a part in history, literature and the arts, politics, personal relationships, religion - in virtually every endeavor undertaken by humans since…well, "since humans existed", with all of the attendant emotions that come with being human.

Over the years, there have been studies done to determine the role emotions play in the lives of people. Certainly, Sigmund Freud, the father of psychology, studied the emotions of his clients, attempting to determine their source. Why were some patients so angry, or frightened, exuberant or confident? Some of Freud's work delved into deep-seated, long-standing patterns developed early in lives of his patients. Children who were physically abused carried on this practice as adults, abusing their own children.

THE ASSESSMENT OF EMOTIONAL INTELLIGENCE (EQ). The notion of a single standard for measuring intelligence, while still held by some in the medical and education communities, has lost much of the luster it once had. The ability to pigeonhole an individual based on a single standard has given way to assessing an individual's intellectual strengths

1

and limitations using a variety of assessment metrics. For example, a high school or college guidance counselor might administer a vocational interest blank (an assessment) that measures a number of innate talents and interests to develop a list of occupations in which the individual might succeed.

These assessments measure a variety of factors - talent, interest, motivation, perceptions, and skills - real world criteria by which to develop a profile of a complete individual, not simply an intelligence quotient. And, just as there are various facets of intellectual intelligence, there are also various facets of emotional intelligence. And just as tests have been developed to measure IQ, there is also an assessment to measure emotional intelligence, or EQ. Other researchers into human behavior offered a wide range of theories. Psychiatrist and colleague of Freud, Carl Jung, departed from his mentor's views on emotions, believing that true emotions were revealed and acted out in dreams, and as such, much of Jung's work focused on dream analysis and what he called "archetypal symbols" - symbols recognized by our conscious and subconscious selves.

In 1920, E.L.Thorndike came up with a theory he called "social intelligence". Thorndike tried to assess individuals' ability to understand others, their feelings and thoughts, as well as to act 'normally' within the society, and more specifically, within the community. It was an interesting concept, similar to today's emotional intelligence but a little less definitive and a lot less assessable.

B.F. Skinner, another well-known researcher into human behavior, introduced the concept of 'behavior modification'. Skinner believed that emotions, and therefore actions, could be adjusted through a program of positive and negative reinforcement, the same principles used in the training of animals. Skinner experimented throughout his career, attempting to perfect a means of altering behavior through the modification of one's emotions. Though well respected in his day, much of Skinner's work today has come under scrutiny from academicians who recognize the importance of the data Skinner collected, but question the viability of many of his conclusions. Today, many in the academic and psychiatric profession discount Skinner's assertion that the successful management of behavior (based on emotional responses) is something that can be learned through behavior modification.

During the years after World War II, Dr. Robert Hartman, developed an entirely new dimension in his attempt to understand how our brains work, and finally, to understand how we perceive the world around us. By combining his expertise in psychology, philosophy and mathematics, Hartman attempted to develop a means to quantify the vague concept of emotional behavior and values through the development of a remarkable new science called axiology - the attempt to measure what is good, what we value and how we make judgments.

"A thing is good when it fulfills its concept." —Dr. Robert Hartman

Hartman believed it was possible to develop a means by which the goodness of an action/behavior or individual could be measured using specific criteria. Dr. Hartman's work in axiology has been used in the study of how EQ develops. (To learn more about Dr. Hartman's role in the development of EQ assessment, see Chapter 2)

During the 1970's, Karen Stone McCown and psychologist Hal Dillehunt developed a course of study. They called it 'self-science,' which focused on assessing and then developing certain emotional characteristics to improve the capacity to learn. The test, for example, might show that a specific individual was a self-motivated leader who required little management or oversight. That person would do well in a learning environment in which independent studies were emphasized. Another individual might be evaluated as a reluctant learner with low self-esteem, suited for a highly structured learning environment. The idea was to slot folks onto different learning tracks based on certain aspects of their emotional selves.

The actual, first-recorded use of the term 'emotional intelligence' appears in a doctoral dissertation written in 1985 by a student named Wayne Leon Payne in his thesis entitled: "A Study of Emotion: Developing Emotional Intelligence; Self-Integration; Relating to Fear, Pain and Desire (Theory, Structure of Reality, Problem-Solving, Contraction/Expansion, Tuning In/

Coming Out/Letting Go)." You might rightly assume that, with a title like
that, emotional intelligence didn't catch on quickly within the disciplines
of psychology, philosophy or mathematics.

Even so, this new area of study piqued the interest of academicians
across a variety of disciplines. The concept of emotional intelligence, and
the ability to measure this aspect of self, had tremendous potential in
predicting future behaviors. So the study of this new science continued
to expand within the college/university realm. In 1990, Peter Salovey, a
psychologist working at Yale University and John Mayer, a counterpart
working at the University of New Hampshire, published an article in a
professional journal simply entitled "Emotional Intelligence." This truly
groundbreaking article was broad in scope, attempting to define, not only
what emotions are, but to also establish the criteria for measuring emotional intelligence.

In this now-historic article, Salovey and Mayer define emotional intelligence as follows:

> *"The core capacity at work here is access to one's own feeling life
> - one's range of affects or emotions: the capacity instantly to effect
> discriminations among these feelings and, eventually, to label them,
> to enmesh them in symbolic codes, to draw upon them as a means
> of understanding and guiding one's behavior. In its most primitive
> form, the interpersonal intelligence amounts to little more than the
> capacity to distinguish a feeling of pleasure from one of pain. At its
> most advanced level, intrapersonal knowledge allows one to detect
> and to symbolize complex and highly differentiated sets of feelings...
> to attain a deep knowledge of...feeling life."*
> - *"Emotional Intelligence" by Peter Salovey and John Mayer, 1990*

Mayer and Salovey continued their studies in conjunction with David R. Caruso, Ph.D, a management psychologist conducting original research and developing various psychological tests. Caruso had developed
the "Multifactor Emotional Intelligence Scale", an early assessment tool
for gauging EQ. Then, in conjunction with Mayer and Salovey, Caruso

developed the Mayer-Salovey-Caruso Emotional Intelligence Test, better known as the MSCEIT, which was a more accurate barometer of EQ. Caruso remains at the forefront of the study of EQ with the publication of his book entitled The Emotionally Intelligent Manager, written in conjunction with Peter Salovey.

Even though the academic community viewed the measurement of emotions with keen interest, the general public had yet to even hear of EQ. That all changed in 1995 when Daniel Goleman published a huge bestseller entitled Emotional Intelligence: Why It Can Matter More Than IQ. Suddenly, a new term had been added to our cultural argot and the subject of emotional intelligence was everywhere. In fact, the year Goleman's book was jumping off the bookshelves, Time magazine ran a cover story called "The EQ Factor", explaining the concepts behind the science and solidifying the concept in the minds of the general public.

Goleman, Mayer, Salovey and Caruso remain key researchers in the area of EQ. There are certainly others. Dr. Richard E. Boyatzis, a professor of Organizational Behavior at the Weatherhead School of Management at Case Western Reserve University, in Cleveland, has applied the principles of EQ to adult development and leadership skills, primarily in the world of big business. Dr. Boyatzis' book, The Competent Manager: A Model for Effective Performance sets the current standards for the use of EQ in managing the activities of others in the workplace.

In 2002, Dr. Boyatzis, in collaboration with Daniel Goleman, wrote a book entitled Primal Leadership: Realizing the Power of Emotional Intelligence that remained on both The New York Times' and Wall Street Journal's bestseller lists for almost an entire year. Clearly, the familiarity with and popularity of the subject had grown with the public, and this is pretty simple to understand.

Emotional intelligence covers the gamut of human emotions and drives, how we see others and ourselves and how well we interact with others. There are many experts, like Daniel Goleman, who believe that EQ is just as important as IQ, if not more so, in determining everything from individual success and happiness to cultural trends. (Remember, there was a time when rock 'n' roll was considered bad for young people. Today, we have the Rock 'n' Roll Hall of Fame in Cleveland, Ohio. (The times and cultural values sure have changed.)

It doesn't take much of a stretch of imagination to see how EQ might be as important as IQ, if not more so. Who would you rather spend time with, a nice guy or a smart guy? All things being equal, most of us would choose to spend time with the nice guy, something that can work to the advantage of the nice guy and those in his circle of acquaintances. You see, the nice guy - the one everyone likes and turns to - tends to improve the lives of those around him. He's a better spouse, a better friend, a better team player, and a more sensitive human being than the guy who only has one thing going for him - his IQ. There's enough convincing evidence to make a pretty strong case for the importance of EQ.

And, what's most interesting is that, unlike IQ, which may change gradually over time, EQ can be increased with something as simple as a change of attitude or a different perspective. In fact, simply by reading this book and increasing your awareness of EQ, you will change, even if just a little bit. You will be more aware of yourself and your effect on those around you, simply by increasing your awareness of EQ.

That's what this book is all about - your EQ, and how to develop it in the workplace, on the golf course (where the ability to control or manage your emotions is critical) and in virtually every other aspect of your life. The objective? To give you the tools to be a happier, healthier, well-adjusted social animal (human being) - something for which we all strive.

MEASURING EMOTIONAL INTELLIGENCE

CHAPTER TWO | 93,000,000 miles from the Earth to the sun.

Ted Williams batted .406 in 1941, the last player to hit over .400.

Kalyan Ramji Sain has the longest moustache in the world with a span over 133 inches. (Strange, but true.)

Have you ever noticed that people love to measure things - the tallest mountain, deepest ocean, and longest fingernails - if it can be measured, we'll measure it. The problem is, some things are easier to measure than others.

We're all familiar with IQ - the intelligence quotient used for decades to assign a number to an individual's intelligence. An IQ score of 100 - 120 pegged you as average, 120 - 140 as bright and anything above 140 was classified as genius, as in Albert Einstein and Stephen Hawking genius. However, there was a major flaw in the IQ tests used for all of those years: they measured intelligence using the same criteria for everyone!

Have you ever met someone who could fix or make anything? Give my next-door neighbor a broken toaster and she'll bring it back to life. Years ago, if you handed my grandfather, Walter Corlett, a hammer, some wood and a saw, you'd have a new addition on your house or a new courthouse in Cleveland. Walter had only an eighth grade education, but he managed all of the carpenters who worked for the city of Cleveland. If you ever get to visit the old courthouse, look at the woodwork and attention to detail in that old building, Walter and his men created that with love and high EQ and, I suspect, high IQ as well. Do you marvel at the abilities of these people? Well, chances are you do, especially if your talents lie elsewhere.

How about the scientist who can understand and manipulate high-end, extremely abstract concepts the way others of us understand the plotline of our favorite sitcom? Or, the artist who envisions the finished work of art in her mind and is able to transfer that visual image to paper or canvas? These are all talents, gifts, strengths, strong points and, most importantly, indicators of various kinds of intelligence. In fact, those in the know (psychologists, anthropologists and other learned professionals in the business of studying human behavior) have determined that there are numerous kinds of intellectual intelligence. The absent-minded professor, who can develop abstract arguments on the number of angels that can dance on the head of a pin, but becomes a danger to others when given a hammer, is a long-standing cliché - one we all recognize. The professor may be brilliant at abstract thinking, but has virtually no ability to handle basic home repairs. We've met people like this, we know people like this and maybe we are people like this - strong in one area, less strong in others.

WHAT IS AN ASSESSMENT?

An assessment is a tool to determine the strengths and under-developed skills of a person. Assessments can measure many different aspects of a person from hard skills, behavioral style, values, learning style, personal drive, multiple intelligences, social skills and personality type, just to name a few.

Normally, there are no right or wrong answers to the questions or number ratings asked of the assessment taker. The participant simply answers a series of questions as honestly as possible. The insights that the assessment provides can then indicate what changes or strategies are needed to help the participant grow and develop.

THE EMOTIONAL INTELLIGENCE ATTRIBUTE INDEX™

The Emotional Intelligence Attribute Index™ measures seven dimensions, or aspects, of EQ within an individual. They are:

- Communication skills
- Interpersonal skills
- Personal motivators
- Self awareness
- Self management
- Social awareness
- Social skills

Using a series of carefully crafted and tested questions, this assessment tool provides the person taking the assessment with a clearer picture of his or her strengths and weaknesses, both within the individual and within relationships with others - the internal and external self. The objective is to create a profile of strengths and weaknesses, areas that are strong, and areas that need improvement. As we stated previously, unlike a test, there are no right or wrong answers - just honest answers revealing an accurate self-image - how you see yourself and how you believe others see you.

Now, you might be asking yourself how it's possible to measure something like self-management or social awareness - two rather broad and abstract concepts. Well, welcome to the science of axiology.

MAKING A SCIENCE

You might remember, from your school days, studying the work of Sir Isaac Newton - the fellow who had an apple fall on his head and developed the law of gravity? Well, Newton actually created a number of 'laws' regarding the way the physical world works and what's interesting is - he was the first one to do it!

Before that apple fell on Newton's head, there was no physics, no true science and certainly no understanding of 'why an object at rest tends to stay at rest' - one of Isaac's laws of physics. The point is, prior to Newton, we had pseudo-sciences like alchemy (the folks trying to turn lead into gold), astrology (predicting future events through the activities of celestial bodies) and Wicca (also known as witchcraft).

So, along comes Newton, with his laws of physics and his methods of study, who can say, categorically and without doubt, that every time an apple falls from a tree it will fall down, never up. And he can prove it over and over again. That's a big part of science - the ability to see the same results time after time. The fact is, old Sir Isaac created a new science and a new way to look at the world.

Fast forward a few centuries to the mid-1900s when Dr. Robert S Hartman, a doctor of mathematics, philosophy and law comes along and asks a few simple questions, ones we've been asking ourselves for thousands of years: "What is good? What do we value? And how do we make judgments?"

> *"It's like chocolate. I can't tell you what it tastes like, but I can share it with you."* - BABAJI

Hmmm. What is good? Well, we know it when we see it or taste it, hear it, smell it or feel it - but how do we define it? That's what Dr. Hartman set about doing - not only attempting to define 'what is good' but then, trying to measure good. Now, how do you measure good? Excellent, great, okay, so-so, wonderful, horrible, awful - we have a lot of words to describe how good something is (or isn't) but Hartman wanted to create a standard - a baseline against which goodness could be measured. (What would you expect of a man who is a philosopher and a mathematician. Of course he's going to try to assign a number to goodness.)

Anyway, back to our story. Dr. Hartman comes up with a new science, just as Sir Isaac Newton did 400 years before. Newton created the science of modern physics to describe and measure our physical world. Dr. Hartman created axiology - the science of values. Here's how axiology is defined in the dictionary: "Axiology is the science of value."

"The word "axiology", derived from the two Greek roots 'axios' (worth or value) and 'logos' (logic or theory), means the theory of value. The development of the science makes possible the objective measurement of value. It is a mathematically accurate assessment that objectively identifies how our minds analyze and interpret our experiences. It also identifies how we are most likely to react in any given situation. Basically, it examines "how we think". It helps us to understand the patterns we use to make judgments. In turn, this allows us to translate these measurements into quantitative scores that can then be more easily understood, compared, and applied to the daily world. These processes determine how and why we act as we do. It provides a common language that we can then use to compare individuals against each other, a position, or an environment."

- © 2003 Innermetrix, Inc.

Got that? Well, it is a mouthful, but basically, axiology looks at different aspects of society, culture and human nature and attempts to measure the goodness of these parts of our lives. Problem is, what's goodness to one person, or what someone else values, (or what a culture or society values) may not be viewed as good by another person, culture or society.

Example? You may believe that the death penalty is good for our society because it deters crime - a reasonable opinion, held by many. Your next-door neighbor, on the other hand, may see putting someone to death, no matter how horrible the crime, to be nothing more than state-sanctioned murder. Two people, both members of the same society, sharing many of the same values of goodness and decency, with diametrically opposed views on the subject of the death penalty.

The root of Dr. Hartman's discovery was in his identification of three distinct dimensions of value (different ways of judging or valuing things). They are the intrinsic, extrinsic and systemic value dimensions. As in the above reference to our senses, everyone has different strengths and weaknesses in how they are able to apply these different dimensions when making decisions. No one uses each dimension, or thinking module, equally to make a decision. While some prefer the intrinsic dimension, others are more inclined to think in an extrinsic sense, or in a systemic way, and the results of any one individual's thought processes depend on the amounts of focus they place on the combination of these three dimensions. Although all are used in the process of making a decision, some are more highly valued than others, and it's this combination of perceptual dimensions (the number of combinations possible reaches over 50 million) that defines how we think, and differs our thoughts and decisions from those of others. So, everyone skews reality in their own minds, only seeing part of the picture when making decisions, evaluating things and thinking about one's self. The key is to understand how they skew them, which dimension they value more or less, and to what degree.

FOR EXAMPLE:

Someone who has a greater focus on the intrinsic dimension, and uses this "sense", or aspect of judging things, will tend to be more empathetic than someone who makes decisions using a more systemic thinking pattern. The intrinsic dimension is one of individual uniqueness. It is the capacity to be in touch with one's self and others through feelings and intuition, whereas the systemic dimension of processing information is more aligned with structure, order, rules, ideals, goals, laws, black and white, wrong and right.

The end result is: someone thinking with an intrinsic focus is much more likely to take into consideration the feelings and emotions of a situation than someone thinking in the systemic dimension - someone who doesn't see people as much as he sees the process.

The trick is in being able to measure how developed each of these dimensions is in an individual, and then measuring how the individual applies them to his daily thought processes. By knowing, scientifically, which dimension plays a larger role, in relationship to each other dimension, we can accurately predict why and how someone might tend to make judgments. And, judgments about a concept, control reactions to a concept (e.g., If I focus systemically and judge people less significant than a given result, then that shapes how I will approach interacting with them, managing them, working for them, etc.).

Our actions are like one big chain of thoughts, starting with how we perceive something, which affects how we value it, which affects how we decide to deal with it, then how we choose to act or interact with it. It is a chain of links, and axiology is examining the first link from which all the other links feed.

People are different. They do not look alike. They do not all sound the same. And they do not think in the same way, either. Axiology is the science that studies how people think. Specifically, how people determine the value of different things; how individuals compare things and how those value assignments either represent or distort reality.

In summary, axiology is the scientific study of one's ''thinking habits''. Dr. Hartman called this unique pattern of thinking and assigning value our Value Structure.

A note of caution; people often confuse value with values. Values are specific concepts that people stand for, believe in or deem important. To value is to think, to assign meaning and richness of properties to something. A Value Structure is the thinking map a person uses to reach conclusions about things. People value to arrive at their values. If "to value" is the formula, then "values" are the end results.

In summary; The Attribute Index™ is a new instrument created by Innermetrix and provided through Target Training International, Ltd. The Attribute Index is based on the revolutionary work of the late Dr. Robert S. Hartman.

Dr. Hartman created the science of axiology. Axiology is the study of the core reasoning behind how people think, their thinking habits and how they assign value.

"To value is to make a judgment about something, whereas a person's values are specific items in which a person believes (truth, justice, the American way).

By mathematically applying a measurable order to this thought process, we are able to make predictive statements about a person's potential for performance, actions, behavior." © 2003 Innermetrix, Inc.

THE ART AND SCIENCE OF AXIOLOGY

The basic questions behind the philosophy and science of axiology are: "What do we value and how do we make judgments?" The questions are profound in their simplicity. It is something that philosophers and religious leaders have been debating since humans could first communicate. The problem is in coming up with a workable definition of good - one that fits all circumstances and conditions.

A loving husband assists in the suicide of his terminally ill wife of 50 years. Is this man a murderer? Does he exhibit a character flaw that might be revealed through psychological assessments? Or, is he a compassionate, loving husband helping to alleviate his wife's suffering? Did the husband do a good deed or commit a crime? The courts are now struggling with this question on a regular basis.

"Thou shalt not kill" is one of the Ten Commandments handed down to Moses by God, according to the Bible. It doesn't get any clearer than that - thou shalt not kill. OK, you and your family experience a home invasion by a drug-addled thug who threatens several times to kill the entire family. You're able to retrieve a registered gun from a closet and have the opportunity to shoot the intruder now threatening your family. Would you? Could you?

"Thou shalt not steal" - another commandment. Would you steal a loaf of bread to feed your starving family? Is this a noble, good thing (protecting your family) or a crime and a bad thing (theft)? There's no right or wrong answer to these questions, but they do illustrate the difficulty in identifying what is good.

We live in a world of concepts and ideas. You may be sitting in a chair as you read this and, indeed, the chair is a physical object currently keeping your butt off the floor. But that chair is also a concept - an idea. How do you know this? Because you can visualize the chair even when you're miles away from it. You can see it in your mind, move it to different sections of the house, and see it in a different color - all conceptual thinking.

Dr. Hartman concluded "Something is good when it fulfills its concept." Thus, if the chair continues to act like a chair, well, it's a good chair. Of course, with a chair - an object - it's pretty easy to determine if the object fulfills its concept. With multi-dimensional human beings, it's much more difficult to determine if we've fulfilled our concept.

We have concepts of who we are, what we believe, how to act (normal) and so on. And other people have concepts about us as well - rude, generous, confident, intelligent and so on. To develop an accurate profile of the goodness of an individual, according to Hartman, you must determine if that individual fulfills his concept - or to put it more simply - becomes the best human being they can become through a conscious effort to self improve. Axiology, therefore, when employed in the study of human activity becomes part science, part art. It provides scientific data (the science part) that are then interpreted by a professional (the art of assessment.)

The measurement tool we use is called The Emotional Intelligence Attribute Index™ which measures the seven dimensions of emotional intelligence. For example, under the broad heading of 'Self Awareness', the individual will be scored on how he/she values:

- Self-assessment: the ability to evaluate and assess the skills, techniques and habits of others and then using that ability to assess one's own skills, techniques and habits.
- Self-confidence: the ability to develop and maintain inner strength based on one's desire to succeed and the belief that one can succeed under a given set of circumstances.
- Self-direction: the ability to design and follow a path to success.
- Self-esteem: the ability to properly evaluate one's self worth.

Each one of these attributes defines the individual's ability to work well with others and to develop an accurate picture of your skills and attributes. But which attribute is most important to a specific individual? Well, the EQ Attribute Index™ is designed to measure how much someone has developed these emotional intelligences and the skills to become proficient. It is then up to the individual to evaluate if you need further development for your job, personal development or interpersonal relationships.

Conversely, the assessment allows you to identify areas of personal interaction in which you might choose to focus, areas that could use a little work, so to speak. Maybe you don't mean to be brusque, but others see you as such. That's something that could easily be identified after taking the assessment and having the results analyzed by a professional.

Take a close look at the two sample profiles below, for Craig and Jennifer - profiles that might be generated by the EQ assessment.

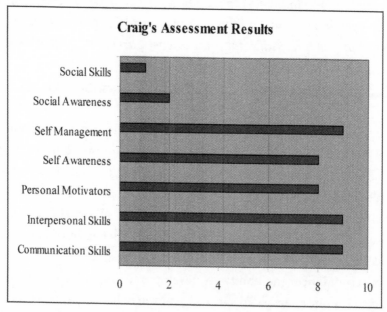

You can see that Craig scores high marks in the area of communication, with lowest marks within the dimension of social skills and social-awareness. Now this could indicate any number of things about Craig. He's a great speaker, but doesn't pay attention to the impact that his communications have on the feelings of others. Or, that he's so involved in getting the message correct that he loses sight of those around him. Taken as a single piece of data, the graphed profile could be interpreted in a variety of ways by a professional.

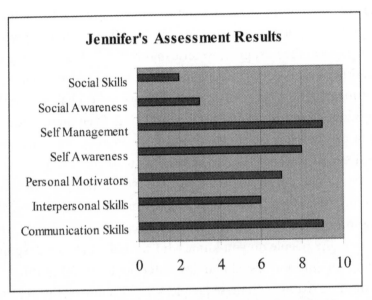

Now take a look at Jennifer's profile. She scores high marks in communication, and self-management. Now, this might indicate a disciplined, motivated go-getter - the kind of player you want on your team. But with lower scores in social awareness and social skills, will she work well with other people on the team who express different ideas or view points? The point is, the EQ Attribute Index™ will add new data about an individual that can be used to develop a more accurate picture of the internal and external individual.

So, is the assessment going to delve into your innermost secrets? Will it reveal secrets you've hidden away or reveal startling personality traits, heretofore unknown even to you? Thankfully, the answer is an emphatic 'no'! Instead, the assessment will reveal your emotional intelligence - strengths and weaknesses - and provide you with a tool for self improvement and personal growth.

WHY IS THIS IMPORTANT?

It's part of human nature to improve ourselves as a species and as individuals. The fastest woman, the strongest man, the best swing - each day records are made and broken simply because we all have at least some desire to improve ourselves.

You're reading this book for self-improvement. You practice at the driving range three nights a week to cut one stroke off your game, or write another six pages of the next great American novel (a little something you've been working on). It doesn't really matter the area - sports, relationships, work performance - what matters is your desire to be a happier, healthier, more productive and well-rounded human being. Even though you might not think about it too often, you do want to improve, and improve you can! Desire is the first step, self-awareness is step two.

But it's not enough to just want to improve yourself. If that were the case, we'd have all won the Masters or the Boston marathon. No, simply wanting to improve yourself isn't enough because, frankly, it won't happen. How many people do you know who started an exercise regimen of walking or jogging and lasted two days after buying $150 running shoes. There's nothing wrong with these people. They're showing the natural, human desire to improve themselves. However, they lack one other key component: motivation.

Self-improvement takes effort, and to sustain your effort, you need motivation, whether it's getting through college or tech school, losing a few pounds or becoming an all-around happier person - you need motivation to keep at it when you'd really rather quit.

No one can motivate you - but you! It must come from within. A desire, a real desire, to change and grow, to renew and to learn a few 'new tricks'.

So, here we are. All grown up, wearing our 'big boy' or 'big girl' clothes, going to work, conducting ourselves in a professional manner and acting like adults (most of the time). But, have we fully developed ourselves? Is this as good as it gets? No, of course not. We continue to learn daily. We mature, gain experience, develop new perspectives as we move through the stages of life - infancy, childhood, adolescence, adulthood, those 'golden years' - as we pass through each stage we continue to change. Yes, you can teach an old dog new tricks if the old dog is interested in learning new tricks, and that's why you're still reading.

Wouldn't it be helpful to know what EQs are required for success in your job and then to be able to assess yourself against those requirements? How about just doing a self-assessment and then asking yourself, "What soft skills do I need to be successful at home, work or at social gatherings?"

The place to start is with an examination of the different kinds of EQ and how we're doing as individuals along life's path in developing these dimensions of EQ. While not etched in stone, there is agreement among those who study such matters that there are seven dimensions of emotional intelligence. And, it's important that you understand them all and the important role they play in your ability to work with others, in your ability to develop an accurate picture of your strengths and weaknesses, and in your ability to become a happier, healthier, more productive human begin. Congratulations on taking that all-important first step.

THE SEVEN DIMENSIONS OF EMOTIONAL INTELLIGENCE
Communication skills
Interpersonal skills
Personal motivators
Self-awareness
Self-management
Social awareness
Social skills

Assessing Your Mental and Emotional Skills in Golf

"He who knows others is learned. He who knows himself is wise."
-Lao Tse

CHAPTER THREE | When amateur golfers want to assess their skills, they are normally referring to their mechanical or technical skills. These skills relate to the physical strokes of putting, short game, full swing and punching. In the world of business, these skills are commonly called hard skills. Hard skills are the tangible, measurable skills, which reflect an employee's knowledge and competencies, such as typing a letter, filling an order, creating a marketing plan or reading a financial statement.

Soft skills, on the other hand, have to do with learning mental and emotional skills, such as controlling one's emotions under stress, empathy, speaking positively and showing optimism when times get rough in the boardroom, a family meeting or on the golf course. These are internal skills. They are observable, and measurable. More importantly, they can be enhanced and developed.

According to Dr. Richard A.Vardaris, an expert in emotional intelligence, there are now over 100 studies to show that enhancing one's soft skills (in emotional intelligence), especially in the area of self-management (self-control and adaptability), can clearly raise the sales and profitability of a company (Connections Between Golf & Business ...beyond handicaps and networking)
– Akron Business Magazine (July/August 2001).

Emotional intelligence is a soft skill. It deals with learning personal and social skills, which are normally learned though the socialization process, starting at about age two or three. At first, the lessons of EQ are learned through external means.

When parents say, "Johnny, play nice with your brother," they are encouraging little Johnny to be careful, to be aware of his actions and not to hurt his younger brother. This is teaching Johnny EQ at its most basic level.

Later, as little Johnny becomes older and more mature in his thought process during his teenage and adult years, his EQ will be based on principles internalized through years of nurturing, repetition and experience. High EQ in most of the EQ competency areas, is certainly not the case for most people. When clubs are thrown and four-lettered words are freely spoken on the golf course, this is not high EQ in action. One of the most important keys in developing a high EQ is how we have been nurtured. If one's personal and social EQ skills have not been nurtured early on, the EQ skills will have to be learned as Johnny enters the workplace. If not, Johnny most likely will have a difficult time with the people he meets and the roles he'll play throughout his entire lifetime.

According to Hendrie Weisinger, Ph.D., author of Emotional Intelligence at Work, "Your emotional intelligence derives from four basic elements that operate like the building blocks of DNA. If nurtured with experience, these elements enable you to develop specific skills and abilities, the basis of your emotional intelligence. Unlike your biological DNA, however, your emotional intelligence building blocks can be developed so that you can dramatically increase your emotional intelligence."

THESE BUILDING BLOCKS ARE:

- The ability to accurately perceive, appraise and express emotion.
- The ability to access or generate feelings on demand when they can facilitate understanding of yourself or another person.
- The ability to understand emotions and the knowledge that is derived from them.
- The ability to regulate emotions to promote emotional and intellectual growth.

SELF-ASSESSMENT IN GOLF - MEASURING YOUR GOLF EQ

One of the subsets of self-awareness is a competency called accurate self- assessment. Accurate self-assessment is the ability to honestly assess one's strengths and under-developed skills as they relate to emotional development. Regular, on-going assessment of emotional intelligence skills will be a very powerful exercise, because it will determine where an individual stands in their EQ, both personally and socially. In addition, the insights learned from the EQ assessment can raise a person's desire and initiative to improve, not only their emotional skills, but also other areas needing personal development. These areas include physical development, career skills training, mental training, spiritual growth, moral development, financial education, cognitive thinking and many others.

In order to raise one's level of development and performance in golf, the development of one's emotional intelligence is essential. This is true for both professionals and 'amateurs' alike.

On a regular basis, amateur golfers have said, "I'm not really interested in the mental and emotional training you offer. I just want to hit the ball better, so I'm not embarrassed at my next golf outing." Notice how these people are not even aware that the true underlying reason and desire for their personal improvement has one or more emotional or mental issues related to it. These issues all relate to one's assessment of their self- worth, self-esteem and self-confidence, as well as the emotions of embarrassment, shame and fear.

Does the golfer also want to improve his technical skills? Yes, of course he does. But people rarely buy a service or a product because of logical, cognitive reasons. They do so because of the emotional reasons – normally related to pain, pleasure, or frustration. When the emotional pain is strong enough, some action (like getting the problem fixed) is the result. And once the problem is identified, a person can then begin to move forward, if they are ready to do so.

Currently, few amateur golfers have the ability to assess their emotional and mental skills in golf. As a result, this area of player development, especially for the amateur player, is often neglected. Even at the professional level, mental and emotional training is still not the norm for all players. However, as golfers, both amateur and professional, become more aware of the power of emotional intelligence as a performance enhancer, the emotional and mental dimensions of player development will be included as an integral part of training.

THE TEST OF PERFORMANCE STRATEGIES

Prior to 1999, there were only a few assessments that measured an athlete's psychological skills. One such assessment was the Psychological Performance Inventory, also called PPI. This assessment measured the 'mental strengths and weaknesses' on a profile that included seven factors. These factors were self-confidence, negative energy, attention control, visual and imagery control, motivational level, positive energy and attitude control.

Another assessment is The Psychological Skills Inventory for Sport or PSIS. This was considered to be the most popular and useful tool in the assessment of psychological skills. This assessment measured anxiety control, concentration, confidence, mental preparation, motivation, and team emphasis.

A third assessment is called The Athletic Coping Skills Inventory-28 (ACSI-28). ACSI-28 measured coping with adversity, peaking under pressure, freedom from worry, confidence and achievement, motivation and coachability.

A fourth assessment is the Test of Performance Strategies (TOPS). Patrick R. Thomas, Shane Murphy, and Lew Hardy created this assessment. A report about this important assessment appeared in the Journal of Sports Sciences, 1999.

What separates the Test of Performance Strategies from the other noted assessments is its emphasis on performance during practice and competition. Research showed that most psychological skills assessments focused exclusively upon the use of psychological skills during competition. This was rather puzzling to the researchers since committed athletes spend up to 99% of their time in training and practice modes. As a result, it was decided that the TOPS would measure both psychological skills during practice and in competition.

By comparing a player's performance during both practice and competition modes, one can begin to see shifts occurring in the graphs. From these results, the trainer-coach can then create specific mental and emotional strategies and exercises on how the golf athlete can bridge the gap between training, practice and competition.

The TOPS assessment correlates with many of the emotional intelligence competencies. It includes attention control (self-awareness), goal setting (achievement drive), activation (initiative), self-talk (self-confidence through positive language), and emotional control (self-control/emotional).

Psychological skills, such as automaticity, correlates with subconscious execution or flow of the golf shot. Relaxation would correlate with the ability to reduce stress and anxiety.

MENTAL AND EMOTIONAL SKILLS AND STRATEGIES FOR PLAYER DEVELOPMENT

This assessment is based in-part on the TOPS assessment by Thomas, Murphy, and Hardy, 1999. The difference in our assessment is that we have substituted emotional intelligence language, to make the terminology more uniform as well as increasing the number of mental and emotional performance categories from nine to eleven.

For the mental and emotional skills and strategies for player development assessment, the student assesses their mental and emotional skills with a rating range from one to five. The higher the number, the more mature the skill. These performance areas are:

- Achievement Drive
- Self Control - Emotional
- Subconscious Execution
- Self-confidence
- Adaptability
- Optimism
- Anxiety Reduction
- Conceptual Thinking
- Self Awareness
- Initiative
- Self Control – Mental

The following are some core definitions to help you understand each of the eleven mental and emotional skills we measure in the assessment.

* The EQ terms used for the Mental and Emotional Skills Assessment can be found in Primal Leadership, Realizing the Power of Emotional Intelligence by Daniel Goleman, Richard Boyatzis, and Annie McKee (HBS Press, 2002).

Achievement Drive

This is the drive to improve performance to meet an individual's standard of excellence or mastery during practice or competition. This competency includes the golfer's vision, purpose, and goal setting, with the completion dates set for each goal.

EXAMPLE: Rita, an amateur golfer, practices a game with 'mastery standards' to improve her skills in putting and chipping. Rita has made a commitment to meet the standards of the mastery game within the next 90 days.

Self Control – Emotional

The golfer is able to keep disruptive emotions and impulses under control by minimizing their effects as they relate to performance during practice or competition.

EXAMPLE: Bill, an executive from XYZ Company, is playing business golf. After the second hole, Bill is four over par, which is several strokes over his personal par. Bill becomes aware of the fact that he is becoming angry. Instead of using language that would be less than professional, Bill takes several breaths and lets the anger go on each exhale, helping Bill to become more relaxed.

Subconscious Execution

This is a mental skill, rather than an emotional intelligence competence, where the golfer has the ability to execute a golf shot without the use of conscious thought control.

EXAMPLE: Just after her pre-shot routine, the great L.P.G.A star starts her transition phrase, which tells the brain that it's time to let go of conscious thinking. She then begins her mantra phrase, called a release key, which keeps the conscious mind occupied long enough to allow a golf shot to happen without conscious interference.

Self-confidence

After building a series of golf skills based on correct knowledge, beliefs, trust, understanding, experience and self-esteem, the golfer has developed a sound sense of his worth and capabilities.

EXAMPLE: Sam, a high school senior, plays his best round of golf during the state finals tournament. A newspaper reporter asks the young lad why he played so well. Sam answered: "After six years of training and practicing, I finally have gotten to the point where I feel self-confident about my golf skills and can trust them under the pressure of competition."

Adaptability

This is a psychological skill where the golfer can remain mentally flexible and emotionally neutral in adapting to changing situations or overcoming obstacles in the golf course environment.

EXAMPLE: Anne hits a pitch shot just right of the green, within 15 feet of the pin. Anne knows that she is going to have a tough shot where getting the ball up in the air softly, but quickly, is her goal. Anne opens up her clubface and with a simple setting of her wrists, followed by a re-cocking of the wrists in the follow-through, she allows the clubface to slide under the ball, popping it up in the air with finesse close to the hole.

Optimism

The golfer remains faithful to their vision during practice or competition by seeing the upside in events, even after a series of unfortunate results.

EXAMPLE: After nine holes, Joan is four over par, shooting a 40. Somewhat upset, but still full of courage with a strong desire to perform well, Joan stays the course by following her game plan. On the back nine, she shoots two under 34, for a two over par round, one of her best rounds ever.

Anxiety Reduction

A psychological skill where the golfer can maintain normal levels of stress and anxiety prior and during the execution of a golf shot. The golfer's body can be relaxed while the mind is able to remain alert.

EXAMPLE: Just before heading off to the first tee, Suzy is plenty nervous. In fact, she's downright scared to be in the golf outing. However, Suzy remembers to slow down her walking pace, and breathe slowly and deeply. She thinks of the first tee as her safe, happy place, much like entering a church. After reaching the tee, she smiles at her guests and wishes them a good round of golf. When it is her turn to make a golf shot, she goes through her 'squeeze and breathe technique', a pre-shot mental routine and then allows her shot to be executed while saying her release key, "Perfect love casts out all fear."

Conceptual Thinking

A psychological skill in which the golfer has the ability to image or visualize the result of a golf shot prior to the actual execution. This skill is applied during the preparation phase called pre-shot procedure.

EXAMPLE: During his pre-shot routine, John looks at a selected target, about three feet in diameter, and begins to see the flight of his ball. Like going to the movies, John is able to clearly visualize his ball on two long strings, extending from the ball all the way to the target. Upon completion of this visualizing skill, John tells his brain it is time to go subconscious by saying 'going on automatic'. John nails the ball 250 yards right where he saw his shot landing.

Self-Awareness – Emotional

The golfer has the ability to monitor their emotions and their impact. This competency includes the capacity to make a decision with a 'gut sense' or through intuition.

EXAMPLE: David, a 3 handicap, is playing the ninth hole at his favorite course. His approach shot ends up three feet from the hole. As he is walking to the green, he senses a feeling of pride. Knowing that this emotion can get in the way of his next shot, David stops, and tells himself that he must stay focused in order to make his birdie putt. David also knows that emotions are non-permanent. He tells his brain to stop, takes a few deep breaths, and lets the emotion of pride go.

Initiative

The golfer has a readiness to act and seize opportunities by raising their level of energy or arousal.

EXAMPLE: It's the last hole of the club championship and Mary is tied for the lead with last year's club champ. Mary has never been in a situation like this and would like to win the tournament. Mary has a behavior style, which is somewhat laid-back, and she knows that finishing a task with a sense of urgency is not a part of her style. Now, however, Mary tells herself, "It's time to win this match, go get it." With a new sense of enthusiasm, she feels a small surge of energy rise up within her...

...well, you know the rest.

Self-Control – Mental

This is a psychological skill where the golfer has developed the ability to quiet the mind during practice and competition events, especially after experiencing the use of negative self-talk. Conscious thought control is minimal or clear, and the golfer trusts the mind/body to create the required movements to produce a golf shot.

EXAMPLE: Paul, after hitting two poor shots in a row, is extremely upset with himself. He begins to talk to himself with very negative tones and words. Immediately recognizing that negative thinking and emotions are disruptive to one's game performance, Paul tells himself to be quiet and return to his natural state of joyful witnessing. He begins to repeat and recite a favorite line that goes, "Joy is the emotion of the soul, joy is the emotion of the soul." After a few minutes, Paul is experiencing a new sense of joy and freedom before he plans his next shot.

MENTAL AND EMOTIONAL SKILLS AND STRATEGIES FOR PLAYER DEVELOPMENT

Summary of Scores and Strategies John Doe

This summary reflects the scores of the respondent as he relates to his eleven mental and emotional skills. The following will give the golfer an overall picture of his individual strengths and under-developed skills.

The Practice and Competition Graphs The two bar graphs following give you a sample on how the golfer can see his strengths and underdeveloped skills as they relate to the mental and emotional skills of golf. By reviewing these two bar graphs, a plan of action, with specific strategies, can then be created to increase the mental and emotional intelligences and skills of the golfer, leading to enhanced player development and higher levels of game performance.

The following scale is used to indicate level of skill:

0 – 7 = Poor
8 - 11 = Fair
12 – 15 = Good
16 – 18 = Very Good
19 – 20 = Excellent

Practice Performance

MENTAL AND EMOTIONAL	SKILL	SCORE
Achievement Drive	17	Very Good
Self Control – Emotional	14	Good
Subconscious Execution	9	Fair
Self-Confiden	10	Fair
Adaptability	13	Good
Optimism	14	Good
Anxiety Reduction	8	Fair
Conceptual Thinking	15	Good
Self-Awareness - Emotional	14	Good
Initiative	19	Excellent
Self Control – Mental	9	Fair

The three highest scores of John Doe fall into the categories of initiative, achievement drive, and conceptual thinking. This means that John has the readiness to act and seize an opportunity when it arises. In additional, John has a strong ability to stay the course as it relates to his vision, purpose and practice goals as a player. By practicing mastery and stroke reduction games, John should be able to achieve a fairly high level of mastery within the time frame he has chosen for his goals.

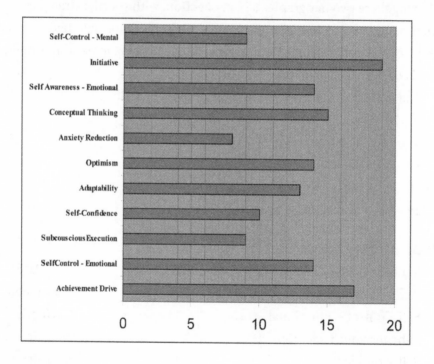

Practice Performance

John Doe's lowest scores fall into the categories of anxiety reduction, subconscious execution and self control-mental. John should take the time to learn about the relaxation response and progressive relaxation, which can help him become more relaxed while practicing or playing a round. In addition, John needs to learn how to switch his brain from conscious thought control to a subconscious, automatic response. Saying a release key word or phrase, or humming a song before entering the execution phase of his shot making, can help him to experience his personal zone.

John can also take time to rest during his practice sessions to avoid losing his concentration and focus. Regarding self-control-mental, John should listen to sound tapes, which will foster alpha brain waves to quiet his mind. During his off time from golf, John could learn one or more meditation exercises, like breathing meditation, which will reduce excess mental activity.

COMPETITION	PERFORMANCE	SCORE
Achievement Drive	18	Very Good
Self Control – Emotional	13	Good
Subconscious Execution	8	Fair
Self-Confidence	18	Very Good
Adaptability	14	Good
Optimism	13	Good
Anxiety Reduction	8	Fair
Conceptual Thinking	17	Very Good
Self-Awareness – Emotional	15	Good
Initiative	19	Excellent
Self Control – Mental	10	Fair

The three highest scores of John Doe fall into the categories of initiative, achievement drive, and conceptual thinking. As these scores reflect the same results found in the Practice Performance bar graph, the same comments apply.

Competition Performance

John's three lowest scores during competition fall into the categories of subconscious execution, anxiety reduction, and self control-mental. As these scores reflect the same categories found in Practice Performance, John needs to follow the strategies recommended in Practice Performance until his goals are accomplished within his selected time frames.

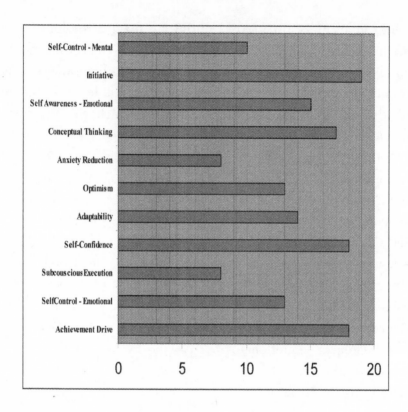

Self-Analysis and Golf Application

Based on what you have learned from the Practice and Competition Performance bar graphs, give as many examples as you can of how the top scores benefit your endeavors in golf, business or your everyday life. Repeat this process with the lowest scores and reflect on how you can change your mental and emotional behaviors to reach the level of mastery you desire.

Example: Title (President)

TOP SCORES:

Achievement Drive (16) Very Good

GOLF APPLICATION:

By staying focused on my vision and purpose in golf, I am internally motivated to reach my potential as aplayer.

LOW SCORES:

Anxiety Reduction (8) Fair

GOLF APPLICATION:

When I am under pressure and stress during a round of golf, I need to apply my anxiety reduction technique to control my level of relaxation and excessive stress and anxiety.

TOP SCORES:

_____

_____

_____

_____

GOLF APPLICATION:

_____

_____

_____

_____

LOW SCORES:

_____

_____

_____

_____

GOLF APPLICATION:

_____

_____

_____

_____

SELF-AWARENESS

CHAPTER FOUR | If you can think back to your days in Algebra 101, no doubt you'll recollect the mathematical axiom: a = a. It's one of the givens in math, because if 'a' didn't equal 'a', there would be no math, no science, no technology. The point?

Just as a = a in math, in real life you are what you are. That's a simple axiom that can't be denied. You are what you are. What's interesting, however, is that you're probably not who or what you think you are! Your self-image, the way you see yourself internally and in interacting with others, may not be all that accurate. In fact, it could be dead wrong. Here's an example:

You believe that you're well read on many subjects - an intelligent human being. You might also feel that you're generous with your knowledge, offering advice to friends, acquaintances and anyone who will listen on everything from investment futures to garden tips. Indeed, you're a generous giving person, or so it seems to you.

On the other hand, your friends, co-workers, family and anyone who will listen may see you as a pompous windbag who never knows when to shut up! You may be viewed as a know-it-all even by those closest to you.

People may see the use of your vast store of knowledge as demeaning to them. In short, you are what you are (a = a), but you may not be the person you think you are.

MEET YOUR INNER GENIUS

We all maintain significant capacity for improvement. Rarely are we 'at our best' and even more rarely can we maintain our optimum levels of performance. Let's face it, we all have bad days - they're an inevitable part of life, so you're streak of 'top of the world' days will eventually end. Expected. The norm.

We can become better family members as mothers, fathers, and children. We can improve our performance in the workplace with increased motivation and focus. We can become better citizens of our communities, better friends to those we hold dear and better to ourselves, mitigating limitations and maximizing strengths.

Two important keys to better utilization of your talents and skills is a realistic picture of who you really are - an increased self-awareness - and the ability to self-manage. Now, you might be asking what these two dimensions of emotional intelligence have to do with tapping into your inner genius, as well you might. Let's take a closer look at this inner genius you have bottled up inside to see how an increased self-awareness and the ability to manage your thoughts and actions will enable you to tap into that Einstein living inside you.

CONSCIOUSNESS – A THREE-LAYERED CAKE

One area of psychology deals with the topic called consciousness. When little Nicole was born, she came into this world with consciousness. It was built into her right from the start, before she was even born. Consciousness, in this example, does not mean to be able to think in a logical or rational manner, but rather, it is an ability to perform or act without having to think. This is called the level of the subconscious. The subconscious level represents the first layer of the three-layered cake of consciousness.

The subconscious is that part of our self which performs instinctually, automatically, but without awareness. The word 'sub' means below the surface. So subconscious literally means, an ability to perform without the need to think on a conscious level. For example, when was the last time you had to remember to make your heart beat, or to breathe? These are subconscious abilities.

When a golfer builds an underlying golf skill that can be performed correctly on a subconscious level, they are able to perform more naturally. This is what is meant by 'playing golf within yourself' or 'Being in the Zone'. When you perform subconsciously you are in your zone and you are playing within your natural style or self.

The second level of consciousness is called 'conscious'. This is the second layer of the three-layered cake of consciousness. Here, the word conscious means the ability to create an image, a concept, or a thought. When Nicole reached ten years of age, she could think about the thoughts she was creating, like "wouldn't it be nice to have a nice piece of three layered-cake." (Is that with or without cold milk?)

Golfers also think a lot on the golf course and at the range. They think about swing mechanics while they are trying to perform and they think about 'not hitting the ball out of bounds or into the water,' this thinking mode is called self-talk. And for most golfers, this type of talk comes in its negative form, 'don't do this, and don't do that'.

The third level of consciousness is called 'superconscious'. The word 'super' simply means above or beyond. And like the word subconscious, there is no conscious thinking going on. At the third layer of the cake there is simply consciousness. It is at this level that our creativity and inner genius exists. In addition, this is where we want to start our journey for becoming more emotionally intelligent, at the level of the three-layered cake, that part of self that represents your core or essential being. (Pass the cake, I'm hungry).

THE WITNESS - OUR THIRD PARTY OBSERVER

The center of our being cannot be defined, because no word, concept, or image is IT. But since we are talking about three-layered cakes of consciousness, we will use the terms superconscious, higher self, or inner genius. The inner genius is called by many names, depending on the culture one is raised in. One popular name for the inner genius is the Witness. We can also call our inner genius 'the source of our emotional intelligence'. It is this essence of our being which is the source of all consciousness, creativity, and effortless accomplishment.

At this level of existence and development, life is experienced as flowing, graceful, creative, effortless, timeless, and joyful. Connecting with the inner genius is our first priority for raising our emotional intelligence in business or golf.

When we are connected to our inner genius (as opposed to our ego-based or ego-centered self), we are aligning ourselves with the very source of all intelligence and consciousness.

The following poem by D.H. Lawrence illustrates the difference between being ego-bound and being connected to our roots. It's called Ego-Bound.

EGO BOUND

As a plant becomes pot-bound man becomes ego-bound,
enclosed in his own limited mental consciousness.
Then he can't feel any more or love, or rejoice or even grieve any more,
He is ego-bound, pot bound in the pot of his own conceit,
and he can only slowly die.
Unless he becomes a sturdy plant. Then he can burst the pot,
shell off his ego and
get his roots in earth again, raw earth.

— D.H. Lawrence

So, how do you get there? What skills do you need to develop in order to find the witness, the core of our being, the one who stands in the corner watching you - a third party witness to what you're saying and doing. The starting point is increased self-awareness.

For many people, the beginning of self-awareness starts through spiritual practices such as witness meditation, breathing meditation, walking meditation, centering prayer, and mindfulness exercises. However, there are many other ways to get in touch with our witness simply through every day activities, such a cooking, gardening, playing music, singing, diapering the baby, or even making love. Each of these exercises can help the individual by becoming more aware of their thoughts, feelings, associations, and sensations as they arise in the present moment. The goal is simply to be present, rather than allowing the mind to shift from the past or to the future.

At first, the mind is very much like a young child. It wants to scatter and move about without paying attention to what is happening in the present. In eastern psychologies, this stage of mental concentration is called 'monkey mind'. If you want to experience your own monkey mind, just starting counting your breaths from one to ten and pay attention to what happens at the mental level. If you can quiet your mind for all ten seconds, you have a fairly stable, quiet mind. But most people, when they first begin a breathing meditation, lose their focus at about five or six. Suddenly the mind begins to be pulled away from the primary focus of counting breaths and it begins to be attracted to the mind pictures and other external factors and causes the mind to shift. This shifting of the mind is the monkey jumping from tree limb to tree limb, sound familiar?

HOW SELF-AWARE ARE YOU RIGHT NOW?
A book that focuses heavily on the practice of self-awareness and the Witness is Stephen Wolinsky's Quantum Consciousness. Wolinsky is the founder of a new branch of psychology called Quantum Psychology.

In his book, Wolinsky describes eighty-five different exercises for expanding one's level of consciousness by becoming more aware of their inner genius or witness. Many of the exercises relate to emotional intelligence, including how to deal with disruptive emotions such as anger, fear, sadness, and jealousy. Most importantly, however, are the many exercises, which deal with becoming more self-observant, mindful, and self-awareness.

HERE ARE A FEW EXCERPTS FROM QUANTUM PSYCHOLOGY.

"Before you can do anything about how you feel, you have to be able to observe or witness it. The moment you attempt to see what's going on inside of you, part of you separates off to see what makes this observation."

" Thus the purpose of this first quantum level is to teach you how to observe your internal experience rather than fusing with it and being consumed by it." (page 25 of Quantum Consciousness, Bramble Books).

The exercises and meditations Wolinsky provides do take time to learn and practice. The good news is you don't have to practice all 85, only the ones that are important to you at this time.

In time, the meditative practices will help stabilize and quiet the mind. By becoming more self-aware, one can then become more focused and disciplined by gently bringing the monkey mind back to center. (You know, it's nice to be home again.)

HOW AWARE ARE YOU...OF YOU?

Stub your toe in the middle of the night and you're aware that it hurts - a lot! Get called onto the carpet at work and you're aware of your bruised feelings and shaken confidence. Throughout the day, we catch glimpses of ourselves interacting with others. Being helpful, authoritative, a jerk, funny, and a good friend - we see ourselves in a variety of situations and, at those times, we have self-awareness.

Self-awareness - a true understanding of yourself, complete with strengths and limitations, flaws, and talents - the good, the bad and the ugly - requires a critical self-analysis of who you really are. Not an easy thing to do for many of us who prefer to focus on our talents and not on our faults. But developing a true understanding of who you are, in all dimensions of your life, is an important step in the development of emotional intelligence.

Individuals with developed emotional intelligence are able to see their flaws and work to mitigate them. They're able to see their strengths without false modesty and exploit those strengths for their own benefit and the benefit of others, including family and co-workers. High emotional intelligence individuals can be honest in their evaluations of themselves. They aren't trying to fool themselves - they're looking for ways to improve themselves. Hey, we all want to be better.

So let's examine four dimensions of emotional intelligence under the Self-Awareness heading, and though it may be difficult, try to be honest in your assessment of how well you do in these different areas.

YOUR ASSESSMENT OF YOU

To be truly self-aware requires a heightened awareness of your good and bad points (we all have both, you know). It requires a conscious effort on your part to see yourself as an individual with specific wants and needs and as a member of the various groups to which you belong. Are you a team player, or do you always have to take the lead? Are you approachable or the office grouch? Are you fair, honest, decent? It's not enough to think you are. A critical self-analysis requires honesty and accuracy. Sure, we all think we're decent people, but we still cut people off in traffic or kick the dog when we get home after a bad day at work.

The point is not to engage in self-criticism but to isolate areas of weakness that need work. For example, do you find it hard (or impossible) to apologize - even when you know you're in the wrong? That's something to work on. Learning that an apology isn't a sign of weakness, but rather an EQ strength, will make apologizing easier the next time you slip up - and who doesn't, now and then?

Assess your relationships with others. Are you open or distant, calm under pressure or a loose canon? Honesty - an honest assessment of the interior you and the you others see - will have you well on your way to becoming a better human being.

SELF-CONFIDENCE

A belief in yourself and your skills. The belief that you can get the job done, survive the latest crisis and come through it all a stronger, better person. That's self-confidence.

Self-confidence isn't about bragging and it's not about false modesty. Self-confidence is the on-going belief that you're up to the task, regardless of what the task is.

We develop self-confidence, primarily, from our successes. If you've been successful in certain areas and over a long enough period of time, you'll come to believe that success will continue to come your way if you continue to perform as you have in the past.

With self-confidence you can withstand the occasional failure and chalk it up to a good learning experience. You certainly won't let it deter you from picking yourself up, dusting yourself off and giving it another go. Having self-confidence enables you to tackle the big things in life while surviving whatever setbacks may come your way. People with high levels of confidence are able to make the distinction between suffering a failure and being a failure - two very different things.

The development of self-confidence will better equip you to handle the ups and downs you face most every day - the internal ups and downs (depression, for example) and external ups and downs (the guy who flips you off as you're driving home). Believing in yourself requires an honest review of your past successes and failures with the emphasis on the successes and the lessons learned from the past.

DIRECTING YOURSELF

The ability to set goals and then keep yourself on the right track to attain the goals is a key aspect of emotional intelligence. It requires a number of attributes: dedication, patience, perseverance, self-discipline and confidence in your skills and judgment.

You know what has to be done. At work, around the house, and across the globe. It doesn't matter what size the scale, you know what needs doing in your life. To be able to motivate yourself to do it and to stick to it when you'd rather sleep another hour, or you'd rather not work over the weekend, shows maturity and EQ.

Chances are, you are self-directed in many areas of your life. You decide what to have for dinner. You decide how to spend your free time. You determine what's important to you and when. That's what grown-ups do. But let's face it, there are times when the little kid inside of us says, "I don't want to have a root canal," or "I don't want to pay my back taxes." That's what separates the men from the boys, the women from the girls - the ability to manage your emotions (fear) and your activities ("I'd like to make an appointment for a root canal). Congratulations. Isn't it great to be a grown up?

I Like Me.

It's called self-esteem and it has nothing to do with an inflated ego. Self-esteem comes with the knowledge that you're a decent human being, that you're obeying the laws, living by the rules and making life better for those around you.

It's the ability to accurately assess your strengths and limitations and then to maximize your strengths and lessen the impact of your limitations. It's not being too hard on yourself when you miss an easy putt or miss a deadline at work, even though you gave it your best try.

Self-esteem also takes into account an intuitive dimension that tells us we're on the right track. We may not always know for certain that the path we've chosen for ourselves is the right one. We may not be 100% confident in every decision we make, but we have instincts - instincts that we can trust because they've proven themselves in the past.

People who lack this important component of EQ often take it out on others. They blame others for their shortcomings, setbacks and failures because they lack the self-esteem required to affix responsibility where it belongs

- on themselves. People who have developed self-esteem can handle the occasional setback, the rough times in life and come through them stronger, wiser, better individuals. Liking yourself isn't about ego. It's about treating yourself fairly and, as a result, treating others fairly as well.

As we've stated over and over, introspection - being more self-aware - is step one in the development of self-esteem. Going through life face first will get you bruised and battered as the years go by. Going through life with little or no regard for others will isolate you from the people you need the most. There's an old adage:

Before you can love others, you must first learn to love yourself.

SEEING YOUR FUTURE

With increased self-awareness, not only do you see yourself more clearly, you quickly come to know yourself better. In fact, tapping into your inner genius actually enables you to see into the future - your future - based on your ever-growing awareness of your strengths and limitations, your hopes and dreams for tomorrow. If you can envision the future, you can set the goals to reach the future you see for yourself and others.

For example, let's say you want to be a district manager within five years - a doable, albeit, difficult goal. But you see your future and in it, you've got the district manager's office. Your ability to see into the future is based on your understanding of you - your self-confidence, your ability to manage and motivate yourself, your plan to attain this goal - all become clearer, and therefore, more achievable as your self-awareness increases.

SEEING YOUR FUTURE IN GOLF

" Danny, see your future, be your future, make your future."
*- Chevy Chase as Ty Webb in **Caddy Shack***

Create a vision statement. A vision statement helps to define the kind of golfer you see yourself becoming in the future. Creating a vision state-

ment is not a mere wish or dream. Rather, it is a clearly seen intention, written on paper, to guide your development starting today.

Most people do not have a vision for their golf game, life, or vocation. At best, most golfers simply say they want to become more consistent. But what does this really mean? When asked, most golfers are simply at a loss for words to describe the player they want to become.

A vision statement does not have to be long, but it should be detailed enough to create a clear visual image for the kind of results you're seeking in business and golf. As it applies to golf, a vision statement might read:

By the year 2008, I will become a golfer who is averaging in the mid to low 80's. **This will be a 15% improvement over the last years. I have a much greater knowledge of my game and can demonstrate my technical skill with a high degree of mastery.**

I am stronger due to my exercise and meditation programs, which include weight training, flexibility and range of motion exercise. **My meditation practice keeps my mind quiet on and off the golf course, allowing me to be more aware, kind and empathic.**

By 2009, my scores will be in the 70's and I will achieve a handicap of 7. **Most importantly, I will experience a much higher sense of joy and love for the game.**

Notice, that the golfer has placed a time frame on the vision, including a number of detailed experiences. By reading your vision statement daily during the first month, and then every couple of days, your vision will become stronger, and in time, your future will become a reality.

FINDING YOUR PURPOSE

If you've never had the desire to be a circus clown, you can bet you won't ever be one. Being a clown is not your purpose. Humans tend to gravitate toward occupations and activities that utilize their skills. If you're strong in mechanics, you'll naturally move toward a career in which mechanics play a big role - anything from structural engineer to auto mechanic to

CAD specialist. We're naturally drawn to those things we do well and en-joy (because we do them well).

Self-awareness is the first step in determining your purpose - the rea-son you get up every morning. If you're a 'people person', your purpose will, most likely, involve working closely with others - anything from sales and marketing to human resources to a management position in which you oversee the work of others - all requiring people skills.

If you're self-directed, chances are you'll move in a career direction that allows you to make decisions and chart your own course - a director or manager, an entrepreneur or business owner - all require the ability to do the job when you'd really rather be playing a round of golf.

Your purpose in life may not be all that self-evident, even as you reach adulthood. This is caused, in part, by a lack of self-awareness. A lack of self-awareness often leads to an unfulfilling work life because you allow things to happen to you rather than making things happen for you. The self-directed individual, the person with confidence and self-esteem, is much more likely to find purpose in life by taking a proactive rather than a reactive role in charting their course for the future. In other words, self-awareness and the ability to direct and manage your-self, are predictors of future success and the keys to finding your true purpose in life.

WHAT'S YOUR PURPOSE IN GOLF?

In golf, a purpose statement defines why we play the game. Our purpose is an internal motivator or energy that drives us toward the things that make us happy when we play golf. And when we are aligned to our true purpose, the emotions of happiness and joy result.

Just to repeat, a purpose statement does not have to be long, but it should reflect several of the personal drives that keep you coming back time and time again. A sample purpose statement might read:

I play the game of golf to enjoy my friends, the beauty of nature, and for the love of the game itself. **I always want to experience the emotions of joy, peace, and happiness as I play each shot to the best of my ability.**

By having a purpose statement in golf, you can remain aware of playing the game in alignment with their purpose. If not, you can always readjust your mental and emotional states to return to your original purpose.

DIRECTING YOUR GOALS

Goal achievement is a process. It doesn't just happen. It takes a well-considered plan, it takes time, determination, dedication, confidence and, of course, that all-important sense of purpose.

We all have both short- and long-term goals. Short-term goals are those objectives that we wish to achieve within a matter of months. A short-term goal might be to beat your quarterly sales quota by 10% - something that will occur in three months or less. A long-term goal might be to start your own consulting business or advertising agency. That's a goal that requires a great deal of planning, a lot of time, and a lot of risk, self-confidence and self-esteem. Someone who lacks confidence will never take the risk of leaving that weekly paycheck. The confident individual will take that risk.

One helpful tool in directing your goals is to develop a reverse timeline. Start with your ultimate goal and then work backward from there to where you are now. Each step is a step closer to reaching your goal. Here's a sample of a reverse timeline for a recent college graduate interested in becoming an automobile designer.

Ultimate Goal

TODAY	Senior designer
7 years	Designer

5 years	Mock-up artist
3 years	CAD operator
2 years	Assistant CAD technician
12 months	CAD department assistant
6 months	CAD department clerk

By starting with the ultimate goal, you can direct your activities toward achieving each step within the given time frame, moving up the ladder quickly at first, then more slowly as you move closer and closer to your ultimate objective.

Furthermore, rather than envisioning the leap from CAD department clerk to senior designer - a daunting task, to say the least - your goals become more manageable and achievable moving from one goal to the next until the final goal - senior designer - is reached.

SMART Goals

Setting goals can be a useful exercise or a complete waste of time depending on the nature of the goals you set. For example, if your goal is to someday walk on the moon, chances are you're going to be disappointed because the likelihood of achieving that goal is pretty slim. In fact, a long shot.

Your goals, whether work-related or personal, should be SMART goals:

SPECIFIC: goals that are clearly defined

MOTIVATIONAL: goals and progress toward goals keep you moving forward

ATTAINABLE: goals that can be are achieved within a specified time frame

RELEVANT: goals that you are willing and able to work toward

TRACKABLE: progress toward goals must be trackable (measurable)

Look over the characteristics of SMART goals closely. You'll notice that each characteristic is defined and each characteristic is earthbound, as in 'real'. No pie in the sky, here. Your goals at work, on the golf course, in your personal life, within your inner self - regardless, your goals must be:

- Specific - otherwise, how can you develop a plan to attain the goal?
- Motivational - to move you forward.
- Attainable - why set a goal you know can never be attained?
- Relevant - with increased self-awareness, you will set goals that have purpose.
- Trackable - goals that deliver measurable results, i.e. self-improvement and increased self-confidence.

SMART Goals in Golf

Just like SMART goals in business, there are SMART goals for developing ourselves as players. SMART goals must be specific, motivational, attainable, relevant and trackable. In addition, SMART goals should be broken down into short-term and long-term goals.

Long-term goals are goals of two years and longer. Short-term goals are two years or less. By starting with the end result in mind, a golfer can use the timeline concept and work his way backward to the present. Once achieved, additional goals can be added. Goals should also be evaluated for their importance and priority. Finally, golfers should also list obstacles they may encounter, as well as the resources they have for completing their goals within the selected time-frame.

Goals and Your Inner Genius

Tapping into your inner genius simply means finding creative ways to improve every aspect of yourself, and that means increasing your self-awareness - specifically:

- Honestly and realistically assessing your strengths and limitations.
- Developing more confidence in your abilities (strengths) by exploiting them in all of your endeavors.

- Developing the ability to manage yourself - both your actions and your emotions.

Self-management involves self-discipline and emotional maturity - the ability to see the payoff as you work to reach that next goal.

- Increasing your self-esteem, or taking pride in your strengths and achievements, rewarding yourself for a job well done and eliminating false modesty. If you're good, you're good. As the old saying goes:

Don't hide your light under a basket.

There is an inner genius within you. The road to discovering this new, inner person may be long and hard. In fact, you may believe that you've already tapped into this higher level of consciousness and possess a high level of emotional intelligence. Perhaps you have. But have no doubt that there is always room for improvement - to increase your EQ and bring that inner genius closer to the surface, where it can be utilized for the benefit of others and for yourself.

Your inner genius, discovered through increased self-awareness, will be employed in virtually every facet of your life. It will increase your confidence, it will improve your self-discipline (self-management) and, as a result, your self-esteem will increase, as well. Yes, tapping into your inner genius is a journey, but the rewards will last a lifetime, making you a better employee, a better spouse, parent, citizen - and most of all, a better human being.

PERSONAL MOTIVATORS

*"An object at rest tends to stay at rest until acted upon by
some force."* - Sir Isaac Newton

CHAPTER FIVE | Place a child's block on a flat table-
top, step back and watch what happens. That's right, nothing happens. The
block remains at rest until acted upon by some other force - a gust of wind,
a torrential flood or the child's finger sliding the block out of place.

Things happen for a reason - because they are acted upon by some
force. Think about it. Ten thousand years ago, our ancestors were squatting in caves listening to the shaman's tales of the sun and moon gods. A
few millennia later, we've mapped the human genome, put a couple of
men on the moon, invented the cell phone and the "Pet Rock". We've come
far, at least in some respects.

So what happened? How did we go from cave-dwelling-mastodon-
hunting-spear-making human beings to computer-connected-digitized-
cable watching human beings? The straight and simple answer is - because
we wanted to. It's just that simple.

People want things. They want to live better, easier, longer, healthier
lives. They want better for their children. They want to understand how

the universe works and what's around the next corner. Yes, we're a nosey bunch, but we're also inventive, creative, visionary, curious and motivated! We are motivated to learn more, do more, and become a better village or a better planet. It's as natural as breathing. We want more, we want better and we want it now.

We all have different motivations in our personal and professional lives, based in large measure, on the things we value most. Friendship and a sense of belonging, goal achievement and success, material possessions, or working for the common good - all personal motivators to some.

What moves you? What motivates you to get up each morning to drive off to work? The paycheck? The prestige? The challenge? How about a new car or a bigger house, a dream vacation, or money in the bank? All of us are motivated by different things - self-esteem, wealth, status, friendships, goal achievement and other factors drive us forward and keep us going when the going gets tough.

Many executives have worked hard and long to be something, someone, that others thought they should be, only to wake up, tired and depressed, when they realized they never became who THEY wanted to be.

The things that motivate you reveal much about what you value in life. These personal motivators also determine, to one degree or another, how well you work with others, how well your personal relationships develop, and how you feel about yourself - your self-image.

Let's take a look at some common, personal motivators. There are others, as varied as we are from one another, but these will provide broad indicators of your motivations and the impact these motivations have on you and the important people in your life.

MONEY AND POSSESSIONS

Pulling into the company parking lot in a new BMW somehow makes all of those late nights and long weekends worth it to some people. Oh, it may not be their main motivation for going to work each day, but who can deny that our toys keep us happy - at least for a while.

The big house, the 32-foot sloop docked outside, the vacation to the wine country of France, jewelry, electronic gizmos and gadgets, mutual funds, gold coins, 1000 shares of Google - these are personal motivators, and to deny that material possessions are part of the reason you work is only fooling yourself. Who doesn't prefer the finer things in life? We all do.

The desire for material possessions doesn't mean that you're shallow or overly materialistic. These are the goodies we expect from our hard work, our best effort. Oh sure, there are lots of other reasons we battle the morning traffic Monday through Friday, but having the security of money in the bank, or the feeling of pride in your beautiful, spacious home for you and your family, also serves as motivation.

A POINT TO PONDER

Many people are motivated by money. If that's true of you, ask yourself if you are motivated by what money can do for you and your family or do you need to possess money, a fear based emotion?

Many people's motivation is to help others. My daughter, Virginia, is one such person. She has pursued a career as both a veterinarian and a nurse, not for the money, but because she wants to help people and animals

What truly motivates you?

The question becomes one of balance. If the only reason you go to work is for that fat paycheck, work itself becomes secondary. You miss out on the many personal, emotional rewards that work-life provides - pride in achievement, confidence, friendships, self-esteem, and so much more. In order for you (or anyone) to find satisfaction in a job, requires that work is more than a desire just for things. Don't believe it? Well, all you have to do is look at the wealthy movie stars or sports heroes who regularly check themselves into rehab. All of their money and fame, all of their things haven't made them happy or fulfilled. Remember, after six months, it's just another car and a whopping car payment each month for the next 36 months.

Benefits To Developing This Skill

- You will better understand the reasons you work.
- You will enjoy a higher quality of life.
- You will be able to look beyond material possessions as a motivator.
- You will increase your personal motivation in the workplace.
- You will approach work with a positive attitude.
- Creature features' (the big screen TV, Jaguar, etc.) are tangible rewards for all of your hard work. They should be enjoyed.

This motivation develops from the desire or need to form personal relationships with people at work, to belong to the team and the company.

Many people work mainly for the camaraderie and personal interactions at work. When you ask who their closest friends are, they will name many of their co-workers.

I asked Greg why he drove over 60 miles to work each day when he could have found a better job closer to home. He said, "As long as the company keeps my team together, I just couldn't think of going anywhere else." In Greg's case, he values the personal relationships at work more than the job or the paycheck.

This is one of the reasons why layoffs and down sizing have such a negative impact on the morale of workers.

PERSONAL RELATIONSHIPS

Have you ever had a 'work friend' become a personal friend? A really good friend? Sure, it's almost inevitable that when you work closely with someone, on the same team, working to attain the same goals, that a close relationship will evolve. It's a fact that we make friends at work all of the time, and it's almost certain that you know of at least one married couple who met through the course of business activities. It's that common.

The development of close relationships in the workplace is one of the intangible motivators that drive us each day to succeed on the job. We don't want to let down our co-workers, our friends. We want to share the load, keep up the spirits of our teammates and share in the rewards of success. Indeed, personal relationships do motivate people in the world of work.

Friendships create synergies - instances in which $1 + 1 = 3$. One worker gets an idea. Then, over lunch you tells your best friend about this great new idea. The friend mulls it over, then mentions it to another co-worker - another friend. Suddenly, the idea expands into something bigger than any one individual.

The key to building and maintaining workplace friendships is cooperation and sharing - sharing the workload and sharing the glory. It's nice to let the spotlight shine on someone else - especially when that someone else is a good friend.

Sometimes it takes effort to build good working relationships that turn into friendships based on trust and mutual goals. There may be the occasional personality conflict, or competition to move up the ladder. Remember, a friendship is all about give and take. Instead of feeling overwhelming jealousy at a friend's promotion, an individual with high EQ will feel pride and share the joy of their friend.

Easy? No way. We have to work to control and manage our emotions in the workplace for our benefit (who wants to get canned), for the benefit of our co-workers, and for the benefit of our employer.

It's important to be a member of the team, to belong, to be among friends. It makes the work day more fun, it makes you and your friends more productive, it creates synergies that develop through friendly cooperation, and it makes you a better person, a better employee and a better friend. Try it and see. It's worth the effort.

Benefits To Developing This Skill

- You will recognize workplace friendships as a strong motivator.
- You will be more inclined to develop close relationships at work.
- Close relationships are based on trust and trusting others is an attribute of a team player.
- You will be open to making friends at work.
- You will learn to cooperate with others.
- You will work to settle differences.
- Both your professional life and your personal life will be enriched by the friendships you develop in the workplace.
- You'll have someone to make sure you don't cross the line at the office Christmas Party.

Our work friends often become personal friends because we share the same goals, we share experiences, and we share the load.

Making friends at work is one of the personal motivators that move us to do a better job.

POINTS TO PONDER

1 | *Do you have work friends that you see in personal, social situations? Has there ever been a conflict between you and these friends?*

2 | *In your opinion, what are the characteristics of a good friend?*

3 | *Does your company have a policy against dating co-workers? Why might such a policy benefit the company?*

4 | *Have you ever had a falling out with a co-worker? If so, in what ways did it affect your perfor mance at work? Did you find yourself avoiding this co-worker in the office?*

5 | *When faced with a conflict with a co-worker, what's the best way to handle this delicate situation?*

SELF-IMPROVEMENT

Most of us want to become better people. Smarter, more compassionate, stronger, more forgiving - the list goes on and on. And surprisingly, work is a big part in reaching our individual, self-improvement goals.

Why do you go to work? Well, the obvious answer is to earn money. But, at the end of each day, you don't get in your car and say to yourself, "Oh, goodie, I earned another $163.58 today and that's after taxes! Whoopee!"

Instead, you're much more likely to get in your car and smile at the compliment you received from your manager on your latest report, or the pat on the back you got from a co-worker thanking you for pitching in and helping out. Yes, we work to earn a paycheck, but there are so many other emotional benefits to the work we do that they overshadow salary, medical, dental, and two-weeks a year vacation.

Work is one of the ways we define ourselves. You're at a party, sitting next to someone you just met. What's one of the first things you're going to ask? "So, tell me Bob, what line of work are you in?" Work defines us. I'm an account executive, I'm an auto mechanic, I'm a teacher or lawyer or truck driver.

And, as we continue to strive to reach our full potential at work, self-improvement becomes one of the most important emotional benefits derived from the work we do. Through work, we gain knowledge, we learn to cooperate, to accept criticism and enjoy our successes. So, naturally, we want to do our jobs better because it makes us feel better in how we define ourselves.

Benefits To Developing This Skill

- You will view work as a learning opportunity.
- You will be more willing to accept constructive criticism and act on it.
- You will be motivated to reach the next professional goal (a raise, a new position, the corner office, etc.).
- Your confidence in your work skills will increase.
- You will more clearly see your potential and the steps required to fulfill that potential.
- You will take pride in your workplace achievements.

Betty wants to become a department manager. **She knows the company is only hiring college graduates for management positions.** **So, for the past four years, she has been going to night school and reading everything she can get her hands on that relates to managing people.**

Betty didn't look at how long it would take, rather she was motivated to learn more about management in hopes of becoming a department manager. **She told co-workers "Four years will come and go whether I go to school or not, so why shouldn't I go?"**

THE NEED TO BELONG

Mentioned previously, humans have a basic emotional need to belong to a group or groups. Our acceptance within a group makes us more confident and secure. We're more likely to push the boundaries when we have group support, and extend ourselves to those within our group. Some of the groups to which you may belong include: family groups, political parties, religious groups, neighborhoods and communities (you're a member of your town, a citizen of your state or province and you're a citizen of a country - all communities to which you belong) and many other groups - from Green Bay Packer 'Cheese Heads' to the Barry Manilow Fan Club. (Oh, come on, admit it.)

Management, what kind of culture does your company have? Do you have a formal on-boarding process to help new employees feel welcome and accepted?

When people feel accepted and develop bonding and rapport quickly, turnover and lost time due to illness are drastically reduced.

The groups to which we belong help define who we are to ourselves and to others. I'm a Republican, a Baptist, a Marlins fan, a Mason, a father and a co-worker. In fact, your workplace group is one of the most important in your life. We enjoy sharing our personal lives with co-workers over coffee. We complain about the workload, knowing that our co-worker shares the same complaint. Our views and feelings are reinforced by the people with whom we work. We derive confidence when accepted by co-workers. We develop self-esteem when respected by co-workers.

Indeed, the workplace provides much more than a paycheck and the natural, human need to belong is often met on the job.

THE ROTARY MOTTO IS "SERVICE ABOVE SELF."

Rotary International implemented a mission to eradicate polio in the world by the end of 2005. This is an example of a big, bold challenging objective that can excite you. It's a mission that focuses the attention and resources of Rotarians worldwide. How's that for a mission.

Benefits To Developing This Skill

- You will feel more secure about your work-related ideas and opinions.
- You will gain the moral support of your work group.
- You will socialize with workplace friends (both inside and outside of the office).
- You will develop better social skills (self-improvement).
- You won't be alone. (Remember, humans are social animals. We like being around other humans.)

Make a list of all of the groups to which you belong - everything from your family to your co-workers to the members of your community, clubs and professional organizations like unions, Legal Bar Association, the Society of Manufacturing Engineers, etc.

Then, after each group, list the benefits you derive from your membership in each one. For example; family - pride, sense of purpose, self-esteem, motivation, love, and a sense of belonging.

An example is Rotary, let's look at their 4-Way Test for making decisions.

The Four-Way Test from the earliest days of the organization, Rotarians were concerned with promoting high ethical standards in their professional lives. One of the world's most widely printed and quoted statements of business ethics is "The Four-Way Test," which was created in 1932 by Rotarian Herbert J. Taylor when he was asked to take charge of a company that was facing bankruptcy. This 24-word test for employees to follow in their business and professional lives became the guide for sales, production, advertising, and all relations with dealers and customers, and the survival of the company is credited to this simple philosophy. Adopted by Rotary in 1943, The Four-Way Test has been translated into more than a hundred languages and published in thousands of ways. It asks the following four questions:

OF THE THINGS WE THINK, SAY OR DO:

1 | Is it the TRUTH?
2 | Is it FAIR to all concerned?
3 | Will it build GOODWILL and BETTER FRIENDSHIPS?
4 | Will it be BENEFICIAL to all concerned?

YOUR MISSION IN LIFE

A mission is usually associated with the attainment of measurable goals. I will own my own company by the time I'm 35 - now that's a mission! Your mission may be simpler - to enjoy your work and earn a living.

It's amazing, when you think about it, just how many people work everyday when they don't have to! Do you think Bill Gates is worried about his gas bill? How about Donald (Trump)? Think he's worried about getting his credit bill down? No way. These people, and millions more, go to work each day because they're on a mission.

My son John is a very creative and artistic person who could excel in many different professions. He has chosen to be a carpenter because he likes to work with his hands and create things of beauty out of wood. He is currently in an apprenticeship program to become a master carpenter, following in his grandfather's footsteps. John is a carpenter because he feels he has accomplished something of value every day, he feels alive, it's a labor of love. With John, it's never about the money; it's about making a difference.

Retirees are reentering the workforce in droves, not because they have to but because of the other-than-financial rewards that work provides. Going to work each day gives us a sense of purpose - a reason to set the alarm for 6:30 AM.

Work also provides the opportunity to make a difference - some kind of difference - in a great big world where we all feel a bit lost at times. In the office, on the factory floor, in the field - these are our arenas, the places where we can contribute to make things better. That's the mission: to make things better, whether we're talking departmental, corporate or industry-wide - the object is always the same - to make things better.

Benefits To Learning This Skill

- Your life will have meaning and purpose.
- You will develop self-worth. (You matter!)
- You will enjoy the rewards of 'mission accomplished'.
- You will feel pride in overcoming obstacles and finding solutions.
- Others will benefit from the work you do (co-workers, family, the company).

Most companies have a mission statement. It's one of the first sections in any business plan. It is the reason the company exists.

What is your employer's mission? If you don't know, ask the person to whom you report. Your understanding of the company's ultimate mission will better equip you to direct your work activities toward mission accomplishment.

It's funny, but you may not even realize your true motivations. Oh sure, you're motivated to pay the bills and keep food in the fridge, and in fact, you may be so wrapped up in meeting those daily obligations that you lose sight of what truly motivates you.

The Emotional Intelligence Attribute Index measures various motivators and how important they are to you. By better understanding the underlying motivations for self-improvement in the workplace, you are much more likely to attain the goals you set for yourself.

THE EIGHT PERSONAL MOTIVATORS IN GOLF

Just as there are personal motivators in our lives, there are personal motivators or drivers (no pun intended) for why we play the game of golf. What are the things that put 'the fuel on the fire' and really get you going? Is it the people with whom you play, the types of courses you play, the competition or maybe the process of learning to improve. Whatever they are, they represent your personal motivators.

Taking the time to assess your personal motivators in golf is not about measuring a particular strength or weakness, but rather, it's about understanding yourself better as it relates to the energies and internal drives that are more instinctive in nature. Learning about and consciously using your personal motivators is a part of raising your emotional intelligence to help you improve and to gain a greater level of success.

As a part of our golf assessment process, we have identified eight personal motivators. Take some time to reflect on which of the following motivators represents you best and the traits you enjoy most in the people you play golf with.

- Body Motivation - this is the motivation to have a physical experience that includes body movement, fitness, flexibility, range of motion, a sense of body balance, gracefulness, and vitality.
- Success Motivation - this is the motivation to attach success to a tangible result, and the need to take calculated risks under pressure.
- Power Motivation – this is the motivation to compete, control and to be recognized.
- Education Motivation – this is the motivation for learning, understanding, and experiencing new levels of development and evolution in one's life.
- Aesthetic Motivation – this is the motivation for experiencing beauty, balance, order, and symmetry, feeling connected to nature, playing for the love of it.
- People Motivation – this is the motivation for maintaining connection to other people for personal and/or business reasons.
- Commitment Motivation – this is the motivation to stay the course in achieving one's vision, purpose, and goals in life.
- Business Motivation – this is the motivation to develop clients and business relationships by using golf as a marketing tool.

Rate yourself on a scale of one to five for each of the eight personal motivators. Your highest three ratings should give you a sense for what attracts you to the game and why you play it.

SELF-MANAGEMENT

CHAPTER SIX | When parents first go to Parent College, they learn three key phrases used by every parent in the world:

" Don't make me stop this car."

" Why don't you go outside to play?" and

"The least you could do is to try and act normal."

What is it about parents and 'acting normal'. We're kids. We'll get there eventually. Or at least some of us will - those who have developed a level of emotional intelligence.

In business today we are looking for proactive people who can independently pursue company objectives.

With the speed of business today, the ability to prioritize the tasks and activities before you is critical to your success.

Charlie's boss scratches her head as she listens to Charlie explain that the reason he didn't get the overnight package out was because he wasn't finished taking inventory. Sound familiar? Acting normal comes naturally to most of us grown-ups. We pay our taxes, obey the laws, play by the rules, and respect the regulations. We honor society's traditions, social conventions, and values. We do our best to fit in (again, most of us), to not make waves and to...well, act normal. That's what makes parents so proud. "Hey, Mom, look at me - I'm acting normal!"

So what happened in those intervening years between shaving the cat and making multi-million dollar decisions before breakfast? We developed our internal parents, the moms and dads who told us it was wrong to steal, wrong to speak ill of the dead, wrong to lie, and wrong to shave the cat. Those values, instilled over long years of dos and don'ts, have become our values. They've been passed on, we've integrated them and we live them without giving it a second thought. In fact, we've become the values that we picked up growing up - during that socialization process discussed previously.

Call it what you will - self-discipline, your conscience, your emotional control, or self-management, it comes down to this: you at least act normal and mom would be so proud.

STRESS MANAGEMENT

Some days you feel like blowing your top, letting off some steam or chucking it all and moving to Tahiti. We live in a high stakes, pressure cooker of a world. During any given day we have to deal with work stress, commuting stress, family stress, the worries of the evening news and the latest increase in our property taxes. Stress is simply an aspect of the modern, industrialized society. A key aspect, unfortunately. It's not like the old days when ma and pa and their 26 young'uns were born, worked the farm and died, never having traveled more than 25 miles from their home.

With stress such a factor in our lives, stress management takes on additional importance. Too much stress can lead to a host of physical ailments - everything from insomnia to hair falling out in clumps! Over the long term, stress can be lethal if not controlled, redirected, or otherwise managed in our lives. Did you get that? Lethal.

10 Tips To Help Manage Stress

1 | **EXERCISE.** Exercise. Exercise. Whether it's a brisk walk around the block or running a triathlon, exercise is one of the best stress reducers there is. And, you get all of those physical benefits as a bonus.

2 | **SKIP THE CAFFEINE.** Caffeine is a drug, a stimulant in fact. If your hectic life already provides stimulation enough, switch to decaf and slow down a notch or two.

3 | **MEDITATE.** You don't have to chant, you don't have to burn incense or play new age music (unless you want to). Simply find a quiet spot where you won't be disturbed, get into a comfortable position, close your eyes and let your mind go blank. A 15-minute meditation mid-day will refresh you like a nice nap.

4 | **SEEK COUNSELING.** If you're having trouble handling the stressors in your life, and things don't seem to be getting any better, talk to your doctor, talk to a counselor, a member of the clergy or some other 'impartial' individual. (Best friends and spouses don't count.)

5 | **RECREATE.** As in indulge in recreation. Take a hike, take a vacation, take a personal day, do the things you don't have to do.

6 | **LEAVE WORK AT WORK.** Don't bring workplace stresses home with you. Learn to compartmentalize stress and don't let the stresses from one aspect of your life contribute to the stresses from a different aspect of life.

7 | **GET A GOOD NIGHT'S SLEEP.** Actually, it should go without saying, but too many of us don't get enough sleep - and you can't make it up by sleeping late on the weekends. You need to get enough sleep every day, between 7 and 9 hours for most people.

8 | TAKE UP A HOBBY. Turn off the TV and do something. Build ships in a bottle, or start building a train set in the basement. Do something that will take your mind off of your troubles.

9 | SOCIALIZE. See other people. Talk about the local sports teams or what's going on in the neighborhood. Talk about anything but the triggers that are currently causing stress in your life.

10 | DRIVE IN THE SLOW LANE. You will not believe how much stress this will eliminate from your morning commute. When you go from road warrior to 'slow and steady wins the race', your blood pressure will drop, you can slip in your favorites tunes and let the speed merchants fight the battle while you move along with the other smart drivers. This is one of the easiest and most effective things you can do to relieve stress in your life. Let 'em go!

Benefits To Learning This Skill
- You will live longer.
- You will enjoy a more balanced life.
- You will be more aware of stress 'triggers' in your life.
- You will avoid many health problems.
- You will be able to eliminate many stressors from your life.
- You will be able to maintain your focus and increase productivity.
- Over time, you will develop a more positive attitude.

POINTS TO PONDER

We all have stress 'triggers' - things that just make us gnash our teeth. For one week, keep a list of all of the things that cause stress during those seven days.

Review the list for the following:

1 | *Is there a pattern to the list (traffic, co-worker, politics, time of day)?*
2 | *How many of the stress triggers can you control?*
3 | *Which triggers can you eliminate completely?*

TAKING RESPONSIBILITY

You make mistakes. You inadvertently hurt the feelings of others. You are sometimes insensitive. You sometimes make bad decisions or use poor judgment. Welcome to the human race.

We aren't perfect. Far from it. Every day, we misstep, goof up, drop the ball and step on someone's toes. It's simply a part of social interaction. A look is misread, a statement is taken the wrong way, miscommunication, misunderstanding...misery.

Positive change does not take place in any organization until people take personal responsibility.

Part of self-management is accepting responsibility for your mistakes and the consequences of your actions. When you say something hurtful, the individual with the developed EQ will recognize the mistake and take steps to make things better. When you slip up at work, don't pass the blame on. President Harry Truman had a plaque on his desk that read, "The buck stops here." Simply stated, President Truman realized that there was no one to whom he could pass the buck. It was his responsibility and he accepted it, good, bad or indifferent.

If you aren't making mistakes you aren't learning very much.
Give your people permission to make mistakes and watch them grow.

Recognize and accept that you will make mistakes, bad decisions, missed opportunities - it's a part of life with other humans. Once you recognize that your aren't the model of perfection, it becomes much easier to take responsibility, accept the consequences, and move on to the next thing on life's agenda.

Benefits To Learning This Skill

- You will learn valuable lessons from your mistakes.
- You will develop empathy for others who slip up.
- You will be able to say "I'm sorry" and mean it. (A very big thing.)
- You will become the 'go-to' gal or guy - the one who doesn't pass the buck.
- You will be better able to accept your shortcomings and limitations, while focusing on your strengths.
- Your confidence will increase as you realize that missteps are survivable, and part of the learning and growing process.
- You will like yourself more (self-esteem).

POINTS TO PONDER

Work scenario: you're the manager of a department. One of the people who you supervise misses an important deadline and you're called upstairs to corporate headquarters. Even though you didn't miss the deadline, your department did. So, what do you say to your supervisor? Do you accept responsibility for the shortcomings of someone in your department, or do you place the blame on the individual who failed to meet company expectations?

SETTING PERSONAL GOALS

We all set goals for ourselves. It's one way we provide our own direction in life. It's also a means by which we can measure our progress and our success (or failure).

Realistic personal goals involve a number of critical factors:

- What is the goal and is it obtainable?
- Do you have the skills and knowledge required to attain the goal?
- Can you achieve the goal in the set time frame?

• Does the goal have real value to you?
• What sacrifices will you make to reach the goal?

You've heard the old expression, "getting there is half the fun"? Well, it can be when you're working toward something you want. A raise, a promotion, and a lowered handicap on the course - all worthy goals, and working toward them can be fun if you keep your expectations real. On the other hand, if you set the bar too high for yourself, if you don't give yourself adequate time to reach the goal, then reaching that goal just isn't going to be a fun process.

Life isn't just about goals and reaching them. If you're always setting and working toward the achievement of goals, you won't have the time to 'stop and smell the roses' or, to enjoy the process of goal achievement. You won't enjoy devising the strategy and then implementing it. You certainly won't appreciate the hard work required to reach the goal and, when you finally do reach the goals you've set for yourself, instead of cheering and giving yourself a pat on the back, you'll only have the energy to breathe a heavy sigh of relief. That's no way to live.

Your goals, on the course, on the job, or around the house should be reasonable and achievable. Trying to do more than you have time for, trying to do more than your native talents will allow, expecting too much of yourself too much of the time, is a sure ticket to falling short, which is a sure ticket to lowered self-esteem and confidence. View goals positively and enjoy the ride. After all, isn't that what life is all about?

SET SHORT-TERM GOALS AND DEVELOP THE HABIT OF ACHIEVING GOALS.

Why not start today and set a realistic goal for tomorrow, one you know you can hit? Set a 30-day goal of cleaning the garage or painting the bathroom. Write the goal down and put it in a couple of places where you will see it daily. Tell everyone what your goal is, and watch it happen. Have some fun with this.

Benefits To Learning This Skill

- Goals will become your motivators rather than stumbling blocks.
- You will be able to reach your goals and enjoy the rewards of success.
- You will have a yardstick by which to measure your progress.
- You will develop realistic expectations for yourself and for others.
- You will be better able to accept your limitations (we all have them).
- You won't beat yourself up when you occasionally fall short of a goal.
- Your self-esteem will increase with each success.

Your success is within your grasp.
You can make it happen when you set reasonable goals for yourself.

POINTS TO PONDER

We all have goals. We all use goals, but for different purposes. Some use goals to drive themselves to excess, working too hard, too long, with too little time for anything else. Once again, the key is balance, moderation. In the spaces below, or on a separate sheet of paper, set an achievable goal for each of the following areas of your life. Each goal should be something that you want, something you can achieve, and something you have the time for. Remember, reasonable goals are achievable, goal achievement should be viewed as a personal success, and success leads to more success, because we like the way success makes us feel.

ASPECT OF LIFE	YOUR ACHIEVABLE GOAL
Professional life	
Family life	
Community life	
Social life	
Internal life (the inner you)	
Financial life	

PERSONAL ASSESSMENT

If you're honest with yourself (no self-delusions) you can develop a pretty accurate assessment of your strengths and weaknesses, and the strengths and weaknesses of others. Of course, if you aren't honest with yourself, your personal assessment is worth bubkis, zip, zilch, nada, the big goose egg.

The reason is simple: your assessment won't be an accurate measurement of your strengths and limitations, and that's the whole point. We all fool ourselves into thinking that we're smarter or stronger, more stable, more logical, more everything because it's very hard to look at yourself, flaws and all, with total honesty. Who wants to admit to themselves that they're lazy? Or an oaf? A taskmaster or an evil force out for world domination? These are not the types of things we like to admit to ourselves, much less to others.

The only way you're going to pull off an accurate assessment of yourself is by being honest and increasing your awareness of your inner self - the one you keep to yourself - and your public self, the one who shows up for work each day and coaches your kid's lacrosse team. Both your private and public selves should be weighed in any self-evaluation. It's also important to note that conducting a self-assessment isn't a one-time thing and that's that. Assessing yourself is a process, even a daily process when you increase your awareness of how you relate and interact with others. Many times assessment tools will show you how others see you and they offer an objective, third person opinion.

POINTS TO PONDER

Using a scale of 1 - 10, 10 being the highest, how would you rank yourself in the following areas. And remember, honesty counts, no matter how difficult it may be to recognize personal areas that could use a little work.

	lowest 1	highest 10
Compassion for others		_____
Compassion for yourself		_____
Honesty		_____
Decency		_____
Generosity		_____
Trustworthiness		_____
Truthfulness		_____
Emotional control		_____
Patience		_____
Respect for authority		_____
Ability to read the feelings of others		_____
Ability to cooperate with others		_____

Setting short-term goals and accomplishing them is a great way to boost self-confidence.

SELF-CONFIDENCE

We've been here before. Self-confidence is the inner strength you're able to summon up when you aren't too sure of the next step or where you stand at the moment. It's a willingness to move forward with courage and conviction, even when all of the puzzle pieces are not yet in place. It's thinking on the fly, quickly adapting to circumstances, moving on to Plan B when Plan A has proved ineffective, and doing so without looking back with regrets. It's the ability to pick yourself up and start over. It's the belief that you will ultimately succeed and with confidence and a strategy, let there be no doubt - you will succeed.

Look at the road blocks ahead and do some roadblock removal before you run smack into one.

Stevens knows that every time he is put in charge of a project, he forgets something. This time he is going to make a check list with the help of a co-worker and check activities off as they're completed - roadblock removed.

BENEFITS TO LEARNING THIS SKILL

- You will be more decisive.
- You will have fewer regrets.
- You will be able to forge ahead when things aren't going as planned.
- You will be better able to take the greater risk for the greater reward.
- Your confidence will grow with each success.
- Your self-esteem will grow with each success.
- Others will come to rely on you and your confident judgments.
- You will be able to accept your shortcomings more easily.
- You will not be threatened by new challenges. In fact, you will welcome them.
- You will rely on others less, increasing the productivity of those around you.
- You will enjoy the respect of others.

"We shall not flag or fail. We shall go on to the end. We shall fight in France, we shall fight on the seas and oceans, we shall fight with growing self-confidence...we shall never surrender."
- British Prime Minister Winston Churchill, speaking before the House of Commons on June 4, 1940 after the British evacuation from Dunkirk

CONTROLLING THE INNER YOU

Hothead. Short fuse. Loose canon. We all know who they are, and perhaps you've been called one of these names. There are many of us who simply have a difficult time controlling our emotions, especially when the pressure is on.

"What do you mean that report's not done!!!??"

Have you ever blown up at work, venting your wrath at some poor subordinate for a minor infraction or lapse? Have you ever shouted at a family member for no good reason? Or the guy at the convenience store? Certainly, there are times we all wish we could let off a bit of steam, but most of us are able to control ourselves - at least outwardly. We may be ready to explode inside, but we're able to control the expression of these emotions to others.

Part of emotional intelligence entails the ability to control your inner emotions as well as the external, outward expression of these emotions. You'd never consider having a 'go' with your boss because you know you'd lose your job. And you're not about to engage in a heated debate with the police officer who stops you for speeding because you might end up in the slammer. There are plenty of good reasons for keeping our true feelings to ourselves, 'bottled up' as some people might say. But what about your ability to control your internal feelings - the feelings you don't show to others, but still feel deeply and passionately? Are you a ticking time bomb, ready to go off at any time? If so, chances are you have issues with your internal self-control - issues that simply aren't healthy, emotionally or physically.

We learn the rules of behavior growing up, during the process of socialization. We know it's wrong to yell at others, or to lose our control in other ways, but the socialization process doesn't teach us how to control our inner feelings. We may feel sad, but we put on a happy face so that others won't know our true feelings. We may feel angry, but we walk away rather than confront the source of our anger. It's not enough to exhibit external control of emotions for healthy relationships and a healthy mind and body. EQ also involves the management of internal feelings - not just acting calmly during a crisis, but being calm, as well. The control of your inner-self is just as critical to healthy social adjustment as controlling the self you show to others.

Benefits To Learning This Skill

- Your emotions will be directed toward the actual source of your feelings.
- You won't have to hide your true feelings.
- You will have greater control over your thought processes.
- You will become a calming influence on others.
- Your blood pressure will decrease.
- That vein in your neck will stop bulging.
- You will be able to think more clearly.
- You will control your inner child.

There's a little kid inside each of us. We may not always recognize this kid, but they show up at the most inopportune times.

Learning to control your inner child means controlling your inner feelings - not an easy thing to do.

"What do you mean that report's not done yet???!!!"
Sound familiar?

POINTS TO PONDER

You can't let your true emotions show whenever you feel the urge. That's what self-control is all about - controlling the ego-driven, inner child inside of you.

What are the consequences to allowing your inner child to control your thought processes?

How does your inner child affect those in your personal and professional life?

SELF-DISCIPLINE AND YOUR SENSE OF DUTY

Are you consistent in your actions and reactions? Do you recognize your obligations and take them on willingly? Do you have a duty to do the best you can at work and in your personal life? Do you have a duty (a social contract) to play by the rules and obey the laws of our society? You may not be aware of this sense of duty, but it motivates some of us to make sacrifices - sometimes the supreme sacrifice. Consider the men and women who have died protecting our way of life for over 200 years. What motivated them to put their lives on the line? Plain and simple, it was their sense of duty to our country and our values and the way of life they valued.

Do you do what you say you are going to do or do you make excuses? You promised the boss that you would work Saturday and get that shipment out. The telephone rings and a friend invites you to the ball game. What do you do?

Where do your duties lie? Obviously, you have a duty to do the best for your family and friends. You have a duty to perform at your best in the workplace. You have a duty to give back to you community, to care for those who are less fortunate, to be generous with your time and your resources. What about your duties to yourself? Do you always come last, or do you always put yourself first?

Your values determine your sense of duty. If you think all humans are inherently evil, it's not very likely that you'll put yourself out there for the benefit of others. Conversely, if you feel that all life has value, you'll work tirelessly to put your values into action. A well-developed sense of duty, whether to a task, a principle, an organization, or the important people in your life, is a key aspect in the development of your EQ and in your development to become a better person.

Benefits To Learning This Skill

- You will be more giving of your time and resources.
- You will develop compassion for others.
- You will develop empathy for those in need.
- You will be able to make sacrifices for the common good.

- You will derive satisfaction from helping others.
- You will develop pride in your work.
- You will become more reliable to those around you.

The development of a sense of duty to others is one measurement of emotional intelligence. It allows you to see what has to be done, and then provides the inner strength to get it done.

In your life, where does your sense of duty lie? To your country? Your employer? Your family and friends? To yourself? What personal sacrifices have you made to put your sense of duty into action?

SELF-MANAGEMENT IN GOLF

You have just hit a spectacular shot into the signature hole of your course and end up four feet from the cup. You celebrate with an arm pump, just like Tiger, and you feel a birdie is on its way.

However, once on the green you notice that you have a tricky downhill putt with a left to right break. You read the putt and go through your distance control process as always. You feel confident, yet still pumped up from your previous shot. You witness yourself make the putt and watch the ball roll pass the hole by five feet.

You still have a chance for saving par, but you know it's not a gimme. Once again, you line up the putt, go through your rehearsal strike. You see the target clearly, and even say the release key phrase you use to execute the shot subconsciously. Over the ball you still feel anxious, and the stress is building, moment-by-moment, with the anticipation that you might miss another one. The stroke is made and just as you thought...you miss it one inch to the right of the cup. A bogey five.

Self-management in golf means the ability to control one's emotions as they occur. In this situation, there are a number of specific techniques the golfer could have used.

The first technique is called 'squeeze and breathe'. When we hit a great shot and get pumped up or if we hit a series of poor shots, we begin to produce a biochemical called adrenaline. Adrenaline is produced whenever we are in a survival mode called fight-flight response, or after an experience like making a twenty-five footer or catching a six-pound bass at the nearest farm pond.

When a golfer applies the 'squeeze-breathe' technique after a great shot and just before saying his release key, these biochemicals can be normalized within a minute or two, instead of taking the normal seven to ten minutes.

A second technique is to walk to the next shot or the green in an unhurried manner. Our pace is very important for keeping us within our natural behavior style. Walking too fast to the next shot will only add to the stress and anxiety we are already experiencing. In our example, the golfer should slow down, pace and breathe deeply from the diaphragm breathing in and out through the nose. This will draw more oxygen into the blood and will help quiet the mind.

A third technique is to keep the mind quiet. A racing mind will cause stress and anxiety to rise. By keeping one's eyes quiet as one walks to the next shot, the brain will begin to quiet down.

A fourth technique is to set a limit on how long the golfer will allow the emotion to last. By returning to the witness (our inner genius), the emotion could have been enjoyed (or acknowledged if it was a negative one) and then let go.

A fifth technique is to use only the words 'yes' and 'okay' if you must judge a shot. A judging mind activates mental activity. In addition, it puts the mind into a state of duality where it begins to think in terms of right and wrong, good and bad, etc. When a golfer can respond with an attitude of 'yes' or 'okay', the mind is affirming the result of the shot from a more neutral position. This helps to keep both the mind quiet and nervous system calm.

A sixth technique is to focus one's attention on the heart center. This will also reduce stress and anxiety. Joel Thiel, a top 50 PGA instructor, has stated, "You breathe through the heart and begin to create sincere feelings of compassion, appreciation, joy, and happiness, drawing from some positive aspect of your life."

SOCIAL AWARENESS

"People have one thing in common: they are all different"
- Robert Zend

CHAPTER SEVEN | You're at a large social gathering, regaling the group with one of your wittiest anecdotes. All eyes are on you expectantly, waiting for the punch line to your story.

You've been in this situation before, right? Moreover, you're comfortable being the center of attention. Maybe you even enjoy it - or crave it. In your mind, you're the life of the party once again. But are you? Really? Or, are you the pompous windbag who always has to take center stage whenever three or more people gather together? Believe it, you won't know if no one tells you - especially if you haven't developed your social awareness, one of the seven dimensions of emotional intelligence.

Has this ever happened to you? You're in a situation, at work, at home, at a party - it doesn't matter where, when you suddenly realize that there's a part of your brain watching you in real time; it's almost as though you were standing in the corner watching yourself, seeing yourself as others see you. If you've ever had that experience, you're aware of social awareness.

Social awareness is your ability to see yourself in situations with other human beings. It can be anywhere, not just social situations. Work, the store, the swim meet, it can be anywhere, but what's different is you and your ability to step back from yourself and watch your interaction almost as an impartial third party might do. You see your sense of humor, oops you're talking over someone else, hey that was a good point and well stated - you're able to assess your interactions and adjust accordingly. Not coming across as warm and friendly? Lean forward a bit, smile more and tell a personal anecdote.

People with high levels of social awareness are aware of the effects they have on others, something that can be used for good or bad (evil, even). Intimidating personalities will quickly overwhelm a less secure personality. Friendly, warm and welcoming personalities will be the life of the party, the heart of the organization, the one everyone else wants to be. People with high levels of social awareness are able to 'read' others and manipulate them, making them happier, more insecure, confused, or informed. Because of this, it's important to increase your social awareness so that you can use it to the benefit of others and yourself.

So, let's look at the various facets of social awareness, how they fit into your life, and how they can help develop a more accurate picture of the real you.

How Do You Feel About Others?

While eavesdropping at a professional event, a man was overheard saying, "Whenever I'm in a meeting with a lot of people, I either feel like the smartest guy in the room or the dumbest."

Think about that for a moment. In a way, it's kind of sad, but when you think about it, don't we all feel that way, at least some of the time. We're with a group of people and we either feel like the smartest in the group or the dumbest - but not something in between. Well, the fact is, you're neither the smartest nor the dumbest, and what's even more important - it doesn't matter. That's the internal you - the you no one sees, except when confessed to a co-worker at a conference after a couple of martinis.

But the statement reveals something about how we see others as well as ourselves. If you feel you're the smartest or dumbest person in the group, you've already assessed those in the group. You've shown social awareness, though your objectivity is a bit clouded by the internal you, sitting in the corner watching your performance.

Your attitude toward others is a barometer of your social awareness.
If you hurt someone's feelings, does it bother you?
Are you even aware that you've made someone unhappy - someone you care about?

Your attitude toward others is a barometer of social awareness. If you think every person in the meeting is an idiot, well that says a lot about the value you perceive from your Monday morning meeting, but it also reveals a great deal about you and your attitude toward the other people in your office.

The importance of an open, positive attitude toward the people with whom you work, play a round of golf, or share a home, simply cannot be over-emphasized in the successful development of emotional intelligence. Obviously, when you close yourself off to new relationships, new personalities, new ideas and opinions, you deny yourself the opportunity to expand your own views, and maybe learn a thing or two in the process.

On the other hand, when you're open to new people (don't view them as potential threats), when you're willing to listen with an open mind and learn new things from the people in your life, who benefits? You do, of course. You're the better for the experience.

The point? Keep a positive attitude toward others in your life. Cut them some slack and give them a break. Don't set the bar higher for others than you do for yourself. Be open to new ideas and opinions that differ from your own. Be prepared to disagree but not ready to disagree. An open mind leads to an open heart, and makes you a more well-rounded, emotionally healthy individual.

Benefits To Learning This Skill

- You will be more accepting of others.
- You will view co-workers as assets and not as stumbling blocks.
- You will be more willing to take direction (be a team player).
- You will learn more, both on the job and in your personal life.
- Your positive attitude will encourage you to contribute, thus increasing your effectiveness and/or productivity.
- You will become a more empathetic, gracious manager (a morale builder and leader by example).

You can increase your social awareness by trying to see the inherent value in everyone with whom you come in contact, whether at work or play. Concentrate on what people are saying, try to really listen, not just to the words, but to the total message. Only 7% of communication is the words spoken. Listen to their tonality, which is 38% of how we communicate, and watch the physiology of the speaker, which adds up to the remaining 55%. Start to recognize your own abilities and actions and begin to recognize how you and your actions affect other people.

THE REAL PARTS OF REAL COMMUNICATION

blah blah	*Only 7% of communication is verbal.*
@#&))@!!!&%%$* *####@?"":@@@#$*	*The speaker's tone accounts for 38% of communication.*
smile, scowl, arms folded, open palms, facial expression, a yawn, legs crossed, smirk	*Body language (physiology) accounts for 55% of communication.*

You interact with numerous people during the work day co-workers, supervisors, vendors, the people you oversee - every day you work with a variety of personalities, skill sets and EQs.

How do you assess your co-workers? By how much they can help you? By their productivity alone? By their sunny dispositions? Consider the people with whom you inter-act during a typical work day. What criteria do you use to assess these important people in your life?

EMPATHY, SYMPATHY AND WALKING A MILE IN ANOTHER'S SHOES

An essential element of your social awareness is your ability to empathize and sympathize with the people at work.

Sympathy is feelings of genuine sadness for the plight of another. We feel sympathy for the co-worker whose house burns down, or our best friend who loses a close relative. The degree of sympathy we have for others depends on how easily we can personally relate to the individual. You're bound to have more sympathy for the co-worker who loses a house than the family you read about in the newspaper in the same fix. In one instance, you're personally involved, and while you feel sorry for the family in the paper, your life goes on.

Empathy differs from sympathy in one important respect. Empathy is the ability to actually feel the emotions of another person. You have sympathy for the friend who loses her spouse. You feel sad. When you also experience the same emotions as your friend, you're showing empathy. Empathy is sharing the feelings of others on a deeper emotional level.

In the workplace, empathy shows itself in many ways. When you cover for a co-worker on maternity leave, you don't resent the increased workload because you empathize with the new dad or mom. You'd want to spend a few weeks with your new child, too. You get it, so you don't resent the additional work. That's empathy - feeling the feelings of another - walking a mile in the shoes of another.

If you've scheduled a conference call and someone misses the memo, instead of chewing them out, send them the notes from the meeting, a copy of your outline and the decisions made during the conference call. Be helpful, not hurtful. You, and those around you, gain so much, turning a negative into a positive.

During the next 30 days pick five people with whom you interact. Pay attention to the things they tell you about themselves. Make a list of the personal things and ask yourself - do I really know what their interests, values and concerns are? What's going on with their families? Is everything Ok, or are there areas of concern? What's going on with them at work, both positive and negative?

Next, make a list of three to five things you could do for each person to help them with a concern, or just some little thing to bring a smile, to his or her face.

The Benefits To Learning This Skill

- You will be a better co-worker, manager, and team player.
- You will be willing to lend a hand (more generous).
- You will learn to respect the needs and feelings of others (social awareness).
- You will become a better listener.
- You will be accepting of the limitations of others with whom you work.
- You will be viewed as a stable, helpful employee and friend.
- You will increase your value in the workplace.

A POINT TO PONDER

When is too much too much? You manage a department of 28 - all good employees, pulling as a team - that is, all except one. One of the team members who has been with the company for 25 years, simply doesn't contribute as much as the other team members, in part, because of his lack of training.

You understand and appreciate his technophobia, but it's hurting department performance. How would a sympathetic manager handle this situation? Would an empathetic manager handle it a bit differently?

No Biases, No prejudices

This one keeps popping up in a lot of different categories, but that's simply explained: personal biases and prejudices are counterproductive in the workplace and they're just plain wrong on every level, or are they?

We All Have Biases.
The Trick Is To Be Aware of Them.

Yes, we all have them, but they do not belong in the workplace. As part of your increasing social awareness, take a look at the biases your carry around - against older people or young whippersnappers, managers or subordinates - check out where your prejudices lie. Then, leave them at the door when you check in for work and pick them up on your way out (or not, even better).

Benefits To Learning These Skills
• You will remain impartial.
• You will be more open to change and new ideas.
• You will be more willing to accept direction.
• You will judge performance on neutral criteria.

Social Awareness on the Golf Course

Some of the common experiences amateur golfers have are first tee jitters or feelings of embarrassment, especially when playing in a social setting with co-workers or clients. If you are hosting a large corporate event or just taking out some of your top clients for a round of golf, being sensitive to how they feel is important.

This is where the EQ social skills of empathy and sensitivity are an important part of playing high quality business golf.

- Before the event, communicate by a letter, fax or e-mail explaining where the course is, including a map on where specific locations are, e.g. location of the locker room, grillroom, range and putting green. Include the agenda for the day - before, during and after the event activities.

- If you are playing at a country club, remind all your guests about the dress code and their need to have soft spikes in their golf shoes.

- Make sure your guests have a chance to warm up at the range and putting green. Do this at a leisurely pace. Plan to have your guests at the club or course a good hour ahead of tee time to avoid rushing and feeling pressured.

- Before the event, find out as much as possible about your guests, e.g. their skill level, experience in playing, will they need clubs?

- Try to create a foursome where the skill level is about equal. Many times less skilled players are more intimidated when they play with players of much higher ability.

- If you are playing with a group whose handicaps scores are 105+, announce that the rules for the day will be very casual. Let your guests know that, if necessary, it is okay to tee up the ball in the fairway, no bunker shots (this helps speed up slow play), and putts within two feet are good.

- When the skills of the guests are fairly low, play a best ball or scramble event, rather than stroke play. Pair up the foursome to be evenly matched. A Hollywood Format, where partners change every six holes, is also a game that is very enjoyable.

- Another idea is to include a 30-minute golf clinic with some monitored instruction before the round itself. The clinic should include some helpful suggestions on how to be more comfortable on the first tee and course. This can take place at the putting or chipping green.

- Use the event as an opportunity to motivate all guests, so they can feel good about themselves after the event is over.
- (This one is for the guys) In golf events where it's just you and the boys, remember that most golfers feel some sense of nervousness, stress, and anxiety. It's normal for most men to make fun of a poor shot. Make sure you know that the ribbing you give out will be received in the spirit it was intended. If not, refrain from this kind of behavior. After a poor shot, it's probably better to try to motivate this person (even if he is a competitor) than add to their feelings of embarrassment or frustration.
- During the round, it is important to keep in mind the slow play rule. Stay focused on the people playing behind your group, and if your group is struggling, be willing to pick up and resume closer to the green.
- Gamesmanship (rattling change, making noise, and other distracting behaviors) during business golf should be avoided.

SHOOT FOR THE MOON, LAND IN A TREE

How well do you evaluate the skills of others? Do you assign work based on expectations of performance? And, most importantly, are the expectations you have for others realistic?

The workplace is a social environment in which social interaction is the business of the day. A social awareness of the strengths and limitations of those with whom you work will better enable you to set realistic, achievable goals - goals that can then be used as measures of success. A team that feels successful is more likely to work harder to produce the same successful results the next time.

Evaluate the expectations you have of your work family. Are the expectations you have for others higher than you maintain for yourself? If the crew has to work over the weekend, are you there sharing the load, or do you expect subordinates to welcome weekend work while you sit poolside sipping a Mai-Tai?

The Benefits To Learning This Skill

- You will be able to accomplish more with reasonable expectations.
- You will use one success as a building block to future successes.
- You will reduce stress levels in the work place, increasing productivity.
- Your department's attendance will improve because workers won't have to take as many 'sick' days.
- You will be viewed as reasonable and understanding, increasing your value to the department and the company.

POINTS TO PONDER

Do lowered expectations mean lowered productivity? Why or why not?

Why is it important for a manager to maintain the same expectations for himself as he does for his co-workers?

How do you cope with the unreasonable expectations of your supervisors? Does your company encourage discussing such things as goals and quotas?

Are there inherent dangers in lowering expectations in the workplace?

ARE YOU A MOTIVATOR?

As we learned previously, we all have different motivators - everything from an expensive car to a new nameplate on the office door. Assessing the motivations of others is an important social awareness skill, certainly for those who manage the work of others, but also for every employee as a means to motivate co-workers.

Motivating others is never a matter of "cracking the whip" because the crunch is on. Personal motivators include such things as praise and reward, recognition, acceptance, and appreciation. It's amazing the effect a simple "Thank you, well done" will have on the work performance of a co-worker.

Motivation, as an aspect of social awareness, should always be a positive attitude, positive reinforcement for a job well done, and positive results that can be used to motivate the entire company to do better. In fact, sharing positive results with the entire company not only motivates, it fosters teamwork and camaraderie as a side benefit.

Benefits To Learning This Skill

- You will be inspirational to co-workers.
- Productivity will increase.
- Subordinates will be focused on the same mission - success.
- The workplace will be more relaxed and 'fun'.

POINTS TO PONDER

Positive reinforcement is more effective than negative criticism of an individual's work. People respond more to the positive feelings than the negative feelings often created by criticism.

With this in mind, what do you think is the best way to handle a situation in which criticism is necessary? For example, let's say a member of your crew is consistently late with their weekly numbers. Is there a 'positive' way to address this problem with the team member?

COMMUNICATION
WITH SKILL

"The best argument is that which seems merely an explanation."
- Dale Carnegie

CHAPTER EIGHT | Communication involves at least two people - the sender of the communication (speaker, writer, e-mailer) and the receiver of the communication (listener, reader, viewer, etc.). Both in our work and personal lives, communications - effective communications - are important to success. If we're unable to communicate with our co-workers, for instance, productivity decreases. If we're unable to communicate in our personal lives, our children won't learn, our friends will become bored, and our love lives will be unfulfilled and empty. So, what's the big deal? Someone talks, you listen. You talk, someone (hopefully) listens. No problem, right? Wrong, wrong, wrong.

Miscommunication is the source of many of the problems we see on the world stage and within our own little worlds. A funny look (the sideways glance), a misinterpretation, an untruth, an unwillingness to not only hear, but to listen as well - all of these contribute to the big and little problems we face each day. In fact, it's reasonable to assume that, without effective communication, there would be no civilization, no science, no art, and very little on the TV.

There are several key aspects to communication that have an impact on the development of emotional intelligence, and by increasing our awareness of these aspects, not only do we become better communicators - listeners and speakers - but we'll also become better people as our EQ is enhanced.

EVALUATION OF COMMUNICATION

Are you open to new ideas? Do you listen (I mean really listen) to new theories, new thoughts and beliefs with an open mind? Imagine that your manager approaches you with the department's new mission statement - to put the fun back into the business of doing business! Are you going to give the new plan a chance, or are you going to roll your eyes and chalk it up to more company silliness?

The closed-minded individual is either very confident or very frightened - frightened that his or her ideas, beliefs, work or other aspects of self are going to be called into question. Thus, they close their mind to new ideas so they won't have to examine their own. Or, they view new ideas with a toxic mixture of skepticism and cynicism, believing that their ideas are the only valid ideas. Both are counterproductive to the development of EQ and effective communication.

It's essential to give new concepts their due consideration. It's not what you want people to say, or what you think they should say that counts. It's your ability to absorb new concepts, weigh them impartially and finally draw conclusions based on your objective analysis. Individuals who have closed their minds to new possibilities will severely limit their ability to improve communications with others. More importantly, they will limit their ability to enhance their EQ. An open mind, a willingness to learn, an accepting disposition are all elements of developed EQ. Now, that doesn't mean you have to buy every crackpot theory that comes down the pike. In fact, just the opposite is true. Individuals with higher EQ levels are willing to listen, mull and, then accept, or reject an idea, belief, opinion, scientific fact, or axiom. The key is to listen with an open mind, consider the communication carefully (without emotion) and finally arrive at your conclusion based on facts and circumstances rather than your expectations of what should be said or what should be believed.

Benefits To Developing This Skill
- You will learn more.
- You will continue to learn throughout your life.
- Your analytical skills will improve.
- Your objectivity will improve.
- People will be more open with you.
- You'll be more popular at parties (Well, you will).

POINTS TO PONDER

It seems as though government recommendations on diet change often. Eat eggs, don't eat eggs, and eat eggs, again. The FDA's food pyramid, showing the basic food groups, has changed frequently. The Atkins Diet, the South Beach Diet, the 3-Hour Diet – fads? Or new concepts worthy of consideration?

How do you react to these changes? Are you willing to give the latest diet a chance? What factors or research enter into your decision?

BIAS AND PREJUDICE

We all carry with us certain biases and prejudices. If you hate broccoli, you have a bias against that vegetable. If you're a Boston Red Sox fan, it's a sure bet that you'll maintain a negative bias toward the their archrival, the New York Yankees.

Republicans hold political views with a distinctly 'Republican' bent, while Democrats do the same with their views. Across the social spectrum, we see bias for or against different religions, forms of government, tastes in music, skin color, ethnic background, status, and on and on.

Now, holding biases and prejudices is the norm for humans, there's nothing unusual in that. But, when we allow our personal prejudices to cloud our judgment and muck up our ability to analyze, we've put a serious constraint on our ability to communicate.

The Benefits To Developing This Skill

• Your decisions will be based on fact, not preconceived notions.
• You will become more empathetic and compassionate.
• You will be less confrontational.
• You will be able to admit when you've been wrong - and apologize!

A POINT TO PONDER

The burning of the American flag has been used as a form of protest for at least the past 40 years. There have been attempts to legislate the problem away by making it a criminal offense, but without success. A trial balloon was floated a few years back to make burning the flag illegal by way of a Constitutional amendment. It's one of those hot button issues sure to stir debate and emotions on both sides.

No doubt, you have an opinion on the question of the legality of burning the American flag. Is it an expression of free speech, one that should be protected by all of us, or is it a traitorous act that should be outlawed, banned or otherwise done away with?

Consider your opinion. What is the basis for your opinion? How strongly do you believe in that opinion? Now comes the hard part: can you consider the other side's position in an impartial manner, without bias or prejudice? Can you open your mind to the possibility that the other side is right (regardless of what side you're on)? It's not an easy thing to do. However, people who can view communication (flag burning is definitely a form of communication, sending a pretty clear message) impartially, free from prejudice and bias, will be able to develop EQ to a higher level.

> *"It is not rejection itself that people fear, it is the possible consequences of rejection. Preparing to accept those consequences and viewing rejection as a learning experience that will bring you closer to success, will not only help you to conquer the fear of rejection, but help you to appreciate rejection itself."*
> — Bob Bennett

HANDLING REJECTION

Not every idea is a winner. Not every report you deliver to management is going to be an attention grabber. Not everyone you ask out for a date will accept. Rejection is an aspect of life. It's not being rejected that's important, it's how you handle rejection.

When you're supervisor calls you in for a 'little chat', do you immediately go on the defensive? Are you already making excuses before you reach their office? Are you quaking in your loafers when you walk into their office and see their, feet up on the desk, hands behind their head?

We are not perfect. Not everyone we meet will think we're terrific - we will rub some people the wrong way. Call it chemistry, a personality conflict or bad karma - anyway you slice it, rejection and criticism hurt. The key to success, here, is to separate the criticism of something you did (or didn't do) from criticism of you, the human being. Because your project failed does not indicate that you are a failure. Because you failed to meet a quarterly quota does not mean that you, the human being, are in some way deficient. Because you don't get noticed doesn't mean that you don't have value and worth as a human being.

Of course, this is always easier said than done. Learning to accept criticism and risk rejection requires confidence and self-esteem, a willingness to pick yourself up and give it another shot. It requires firm convictions, but a willingness to learn and adjust. In short, when you put yourself out there where your work, your ideas, your self-image can be judged, evaluated, criticized and even rejected. It takes guts, fortitude, maturity and a positive attitude. It's not easy to stick your neck out, to take the risk and be willing to accept the criticism that comes your way. But, through the development of EQ, you will quickly come to see the distinction between criticism of an action and criticism of you, the human being.

Benefits To Developing This Skill
- You will be willing to take more (prudent) risks.
- You will learn from your mistakes. (The best lessons are learned from our failures, not our successes.)
- You will learn from others.
- You will develop self-confidence.
- You will accept constructive criticism in the spirit it's intended.
- You will learn to trust the judgment of others (and let things go).

A POINT TO PONDER

You've got this great idea for an Internet, e-tail store catering to people who keep hamsters for pets - designer clothes for rodents! But everybody tells you you're nuts. Your wife thinks you're crazy, your dad won't loan you the start up money and even your kids laugh at your plan.

How do you think you'd react to the reactions of those around you? Would you give up without trying? Would your self-confidence be tested, or would it enable you to move ahead despite the criticism all around you?

Are you willing to chart your own course in the face of criticism and rejection? If not, is it still possible to reach your full potential?

TIMING IS EVERYTHING

You're in a departmental meeting with 10 of your co-workers. The topic du jour is the new reporting procedures that upper management wants to implement. Then, about 10 minutes into the meeting, Jerry asks, "What about those new laptops we were promised?" Thanks, Jer, you just asked the right question - at the wrong time!

The meeting is about reporting procedures, not the promised new hardware, and good ol' Jerry just threw a monkey wrench into the mix by moving 'off topic', a no-no in the business world and in your personal life.

You arrive home after a hard day at the office. Your husband is in the kitchen trying to get supper on the table for two screaming kids. The house is a shambles, your husband is frazzled to the max, the kids are coping with sugar overload and you ask, "When are we going to be able to buy a new car? I'm tired of the old one." Talk about bad timing. Wrong time, wrong place, and wrong question. When communicating, timing is everything.

Timing your questions and comments make them more effective, more compelling, more accurate, and more considered. Start by considering the current circumstances. Does the person to whom you wish to speak have a quiet moment, a moment to focus on you and you alone? Obviously the overworked father mentioned above was thinking about anything but the new car issue. The wife, who brought up the question of the new car, was insensitive to her husband's circumstances, and in this case, you can be sure that she isn't going to get the answer she's looking for. Even though she was correct they do need a new car, and soon, the timing was all-wrong.

You think you deserve a raise, and you want to discuss the matter with your boss. So, while discussing a shipping problem, you blurt out, "Steve, I think I deserve a raise." Naturally, Steve is taken aback by your statement, assumes it is somehow related to the shipping problem under discussion and, frankly, just doesn't see the connection. Your chances of getting that raise are greatly improved if: (1) you've thought out your position, put together your arguments for a raise and you've rehearsed what you're going to say and, (2) you set up an appointment with your boss to discuss the matter. This way, you can be sure that both you and Steve are on the same page, not talking past each other.

Timing is everything. Choose your opportunities carefully, and then exploit them fully. Make sure that you're properly prepared for the discussion and your listener is in the right mindset to listen. An improved sense of when to speak will make you a more effective communicator.

Benefits To Developing This Skill
- You and your listener will be talking about the same things.
- Your listener will be more inclined to listen.
- You will have time to clarify your thoughts in your own mind. You can even write them down, if you think that will help.
- Your message is more likely to be heard and understood.
- Your ability to communicate with focus and accuracy will improve.

POINTS TO PONDER

Saying the right thing at the right time is what timing is all about. But how do you know when the time is right? Well, consider the nature of the question or comment. Consider the circumstances of your listener (busy, pressured, tired, happy). And finally, weigh your expectations for the response you want.

You're the shift manager and you've noticed that one of the assemblers is under performing. You know he's having troubles at home, but you can only be sympathetic for so long before your manager starts asking questions. How would you approach this delicate situation? You don't want to lose the assembler (you're short-handed as it is) and you sympathize with the worker's personal problem. When would be the best time to discuss the need for increased productivity?

ASSESSING THE ATTITUDE OF YOUR LISTENER
When we think of communicating with others, we usually think in terms of the exchange of words, but, in fact, words are simply one means

of communicating with others. A raised eyebrow, a smile, the position of the hands - all of these are forms of non-verbal communication. A raised eyebrow might indicate surprise, skepticism or disbelief. A smile might indicate acceptance or agreement. Hands folded might indicate interest. The ability to 'read' the body language of others is an important dimension of effective communication.

Facial expressions will often reveal the attitude of the speaker and listener. If someone is 'in your face', poking you in the arm with his finger for emphasis, it's not hard to figure out the attitude of the speaker - he's angry! And apparently very angry. On the other hand, someone who leans back in his chair, hands behind head, is relaxed, calm, and maybe even confident in what he's saying.

When communicating with others, don't just focus on the words they're saying. Check out their posture (closed and protective or open and willing), their facial expressions, their eyes (are they looking right at you or are eyes cast downward, or darting to avoid looking at you), and hand gestures (hands up resisting you or open to your new idea).

Benefits To Developing This Skill

- By reading body language, the person with whom you're speaking will reveal their true feelings, which may not be reflected in the words they speak.
- You will become more sensitive to the feelings of others.
- You will be able to better assess the attitude of the listener or speaker.
- You will be able to adjust your attitude and your communications based on the attitude of the other individual.
- You will be able to react in an appropriate manner.
- You will become more aware of your own body language.
- You will be better equipped to manage your body language to send the message you want or intend to send.
- You will develop a better (more accurate) understanding of what is really being said, i.e., reading between the lines.

POINTS TO PONDER

What do the following examples of communication tell you about an individual?

Darting eyes _____

Legs crossed _____

Leaning forward _____

A big smile _____

Yelling _____

Tapping foot _____

Arms folded _____

Finger pointing _____

INTERPERSONAL SKILLS

"Modeling great performers in business and golf is a sure way to a winning strategy. " *- John M. Bothwell, Ph.D.*

CHAPTER NINE | Synergy.

1 + 1 = 3.

The whole is greater than the sum of the parts.

That's the result when people effectively utilize their interpersonal skills. Interpersonal skills involve your ability to work closely with others, to cooperate and to be either a leader or follower when circumstances call for one or the other.

Is there a 'control freak' in your office, or workplace - someone who has to run things in virtually every situation? This person believes that no one can do the job as well as he can. This person lacks confidence in those with whom he works or lives. This person is also more likely to be on edge, stressed out and even aggressive in his actions or words. This person needs to focus on those all-important, interpersonal skills to avoid blowing out an aorta.

Do you have expectations of perfection? Perfection from yourself and others? Do you think life should always run smoothly if you just plan ahead and keep on course? Let's face it, there's a bit of that in all of us. But, are your expectations realistic? Are your objectives actually attainable or are you constantly swimming upstream?

What about delegating responsibility or authority? Are you able to let someone else do it while you move on to other things - or are you that control freak previously mentioned? Let's take a closer look at key, inter-personal skills to see where you stand when it comes to 'playing well with others' in the world of grownups.

YOUR ATTITUDE TOWARD OTHERS

Think you're always right? Well, maybe you're not. Think you're al-ways wrong? Not so. Your attitude toward others - their opinions, their ideas and beliefs, their aspirations and needs - your attitude toward all of these things is a major factor in how well you interact with co-workers, members of the family and people you meet and greet in the streets of your community.

Of course, your attitude toward others is a direct correlation of your attitude toward yourself. If you think you're 'all that', you won't be open to new ideas because your ideas will always be better. Feel like a failure? Lack confidence? Then, you'll be the proverbial doormat that others walk all over. How you feel about yourself will determine how you feel about others. It will also have a strong bearing on who the other people are that you attract into your life.

The desired result is an individual who can be open to new suggestions and ideas, and honest and impartial in assessing them. A cooperative co-worker, a supportive spouse, an understanding friend - that's what results from a positive attitude toward others.

"Great accomplishments have resulted from the transmission of ideas and enthusiasm." - Thomas J. Watson

---

Benefits To Developing This Skill

- You will be open to new ideas and thus, will learn more.
- You will develop empathy for others.
- You will be able to work with others more effectively.
- Your productivity will increase, doing more in less time.
- You will eliminate some of the stressors in your life.
- You will have more fun when cooperating with others. (And shouldn't life be fun?)
- Your objectivity will increase, enabling you to make clear-headed decisions based on fact and circumstance.
- You will develop confidence in those around you.
- You will develop a support network - a group of people in your life that will provide emotional support when you need it (We all need a little emotional support at some time.)
- Your positive attitude will spread to others, improving their lives.
- You will become a better co-worker, spouse, friend and overall human being by maintaining a positive attitude.

I had the pleasure of working for a manager early in my career who always seemed to be able to identify a person's strengths and play to those strengths. I asked him one day how he did it and he said it was quite simple. He tried to bring out the best in everybody and let the team and individuals share in the glory even if it meant he had to step back. I learned from this man that successful relationships are built on mutual trust and respect, and not to superimpose my values on others.

POINTS TO PONDER

Do you maintain a positive attitude with regard to your work and home life? Are you the eternal optimist? What are the positives in maintaining a positive attitude? In what ways do you limit yourself by looking for the negative or downside to the events in your life?

CONTROLLING YOUR PREJUDICES

Your biases and prejudices (we all have them) will limit your ability to work well with others. Perhaps you think that women are, by nature, illogical or that all men are pigs. You might feel that the new kid, right out of school, doesn't have anything to offer in the way of new ideas, or that the old guy in the back cubicle is nothing but a 'feeb'.

Prejudices are both learned and acquired through experience. If you grew up in a home where racial prejudice was openly expressed, chances are you'll express racial prejudice, or at least maintain a bias against a particular race or ethnic group. This is a learned prejudice since it has no basis in reality.

An acquired prejudice is one that develops from experience. If an individual grows up in a home where his opinions are routinely ridiculed, that person might develop a prejudice against authority figures (who never listen anyway). That's an acquired prejudice - something learned through experience.

Prejudice is an unfounded belief that a group of people are universally endowed with the same characteristics. This ethnic group is stupid, this racial group is violent, this age group has nothing useful to say, this gender is aggressive - as soon as you clump together all members of any group, guess what? You're expressing a personal prejudice.

Your biases and prejudices cloud your judgment and your ability to think clearly and logically. Prejudices close your mind to new ideas and new people. The ability to control your prejudices - to eliminate them from your thinking and assessment processes - equips you to listen with an open mind, something that will improve your ability to cooperate and be a real team player, whether the team is the crew at work, your family, or the team that makes up your neighborhood and community. Prejudice narrows your focus; a lack of prejudice expands your horizons.

Benefits To Developing This Skill

- You will be more open to new ideas and views.
- You will be able to assess a concept or an individual on merit, not preconceived notions.

- Your beliefs will be grounded in reality, not perception.
- You will treat people fairly and, in turn, they will treat you fairly.
- You will increase cooperation and facilitate synergy (1 + 1 = 3).

A POINT TO PONDER

One of the most basic of human emotional needs is to belong - to be a part of a group where you're accepted and supported, where you can be yourself. This need to belong is, in part, behind the human need to form groups. You're a member of a family group, a work group, perhaps a service club or sports team. Think about all of the groups to which you belong. How does belonging to these different groups make you feel? More confident? Accepted by others? Secure?

BEING REALISTIC

"Get real!"

Ever heard that before? No doubt, you have. We all have, usually when we express an idea or thought that isn't realistic in the mind of the speaker of those words. "I think we should sell all of our stuff and move to Tahiti!" you announce one evening over dinner, to which your family replies, in unison, "Get real!" Hey, what'd you expect when you drop such a bombshell?

Like dogs in a wheel, birds in a cage, or squirrels in a chain, ambitious men still climb and climb, with great labor, and incessant anxiety, but never reach the top. - Robert Browning

Setting realistic goals for yourself and others, having realistic expectations of those in your life, may not always be easy - especially when you, the proud parent, believe that your son is going to be the next big thing in the NBA. Get real!

Realistic goals and expectation are goals that can actually be achieved and expectations that can actually be met - in the real world. No pie-in-the-sky quarterly sales quotas, no mistaken beliefs that people enjoy working on weekends, no NBA for your sports-challenged offspring.

Instead, by setting achievable goals for yourself and others, you can develop a workable plan to reach those goals and meet expectations. You can provide incentive and motivation, reward the good effort and lighten up on the human race - and yourself.

Realistic goals and reasonable expectations will also keep you from constant disappointment in those around you, and disappointment in yourself. So get real and get more out of your work and your personal life.

Benefits To Developing This Skill

- Success will be achievable.
- Setting goals will become easier.
- Developing a workable plan for goal achievement becomes simpler.
- You will be a more effective manager.
- You will be able to reward success in yourself and in others.
- You will be able to better assess your progress and the progress of others.
- You will be better equipped to assess the strengths and limitations of those around you.
- You will avoid constant disappointment.

POINTS TO PONDER

1. Do you have goals - both short- and long-term goals? On what do you base your goals?

2. Do you believe your goals are achievable? If so, why do you believe this?

3. Do you have expectations of others? Are your expectations for others consistent with your expectations for yourself?

4. Do you think lowering your expectations indicates lowered performance on your part or on the part of those you manage? Why or why not?

How do you measure your success?

GIVING UP CONTROL

Are you the only one who can do it right? Many of us feel that way. We're not ready, willing and/or able to assign responsibility or control to others in our family or with whom we work. This often leaves us over-worked and under-appreciated, at least as we see things.

Giving up control of a workplace assignment requires confidence in those around you. You must be able to accurately assess individual strengths and limitations of co-workers, determine who is best suited to handle the job, make the assignment and then (this is the important part) walk away. You must develop the ability to leave the responsibility with someone else.

The same thing is true in virtually all of your personal relationships. You can't do it all, you can't have it all. Having it all - the satisfying career, the "Leave It To Beaver" home life, an active social life, money in the bank, well-adjusted kids - having it all is a myth, a remnant left over from the '60s and '70s when women were leaving the homestead and entering the workplace. It's essential to assign some of your assumed responsibilities to others in order to simply survive in the work-a-day world and in your fast-paced, supercharged personal life.

Benefits To Developing This Skill

- You will be able to better pace yourself.
- You won't be a stumbling block to the work of others.
- You will increase your awareness of the strengths and limitations of key people in your life.
- You will develop trust in the abilities of those around you.

- Your individual productivity will increase.
- You will find the time to exhale.
- You will be better prepared to accept your own limitations (a good thing).
- The people around you will be given the opportunity to succeed.
- The people around you will feel trusted and respected.

POINTS TO PONDER

In what ways do 'control freaks' hinder the work of others?

How are controlling people seen by others? (Think about the control freaks in your life and how you feel about them!)

Why are some people unable to give up control? What does it take to do so?

What are some of the potential pitfalls and dangers of assigning responsibilities to others? How can doing so backfire?

How Well Do You Work With Others?

SOCIAL SKILLS

CHAPTER TEN | John Updike observed that "Golf appeals to the idiot in us and the child. Just how childlike golf players become is proven by their frequent inability to count past five."

"Mind your manners young man!" "It's not polite to stare, dear." "Always hold the door for the person following you."

Yes, we all learned good manners from mom and dad, but have we fully integrated these social skills into our emotional intelligence. Surprisingly, many so-called adults haven't. Oh, they may look like adults, wear grown-up clothes and drive a big old car. They may oversee the work of hundreds of people every day and manage a $50 million budget to the penny. But they sometimes interact with others in their rebellious child and critical parent ego state.

These are the people you avoid when possible. The people we laugh at in "Dilbert" each morning. Now the question is: are you one of them? How would you know? Is a subordinate going to march up and tell you you're acting like a five-year-old? Not very likely. And as long as your department's numbers are met each month, the folks on the top floor don't care how you get the job done; or do they. Chances are, you're going to have to discover if you're socially challenged at work all on your own. Here's how:

CONTROLLING YOUR EMOTIONS

Yes, we've all been here before, because, again controlling one's emotions is an aspect of several dimensions of emotional intelligence.

To what extent are you able to remain calm and rational in your thinking when the pressure is on, or when things in the workplace (or on the course) aren't going your way? Are you able to manage the stress and keep your mind functioning clearly and logically at all times? There are certain physical activities - a brisk walk, or a moment of quiet meditation in a darkened room - that can be very useful in centering yourself, calming the jitters and getting your thinking processes back to where they should be. It may seem difficult at first, but with an increased awareness of the problem and practice, you will be better equipped to manage stress and setbacks, regardless of when and where they occur in your life.

Benefits To Learning This Skill

- You will be more effective under stress.
- You will be able to use stress as a motivator - a positive, not a negative.
- You will behave objectively, rather than emotionally, increasing your rational thinking skills.
- Your productivity will increase.
- Your co-workers will be able to rely on you when the going gets tough.
- You will meet with greater success in the workplace and on the course.
- Management of emotions does not mean the elimination of emotions. Thus, you will respond with the appropriate response when faced with an emotional stimulus but you will chose the response vs. your emotions controlling you.

A POINT TO PONDER

Stress is a part of work life, whether we're sitting at a big desk on the top floor, or trying to get all of the mail delivered before noon.

What steps can you take to elicit the appropriate emotional response when faced with work stress? How can you better prepare yourself to handle routine work stress, knowing that it's an aspect of your job?

HELPING OTHERS TO DEVELOP

Whether you're a manager, a supervisor, the CEO of a Fortune 500 company, or a motivated co-worker, the development of your EQ will help to bring out the best in others with whom you work - and do it without sounding like a know-it-all.

The key is in developing your ability to assess the strengths and limitations of others, what their motivations are, and how to effectively exploit strengths and personal motivators while mitigating the effect of limitations and shortcomings. Your ability to do this requires that you be able to empathize with those with whom you work, to get inside their minds to truly understand what makes them tick - not always an easy thing to do.

However, by spending time with your co-workers, getting to know about their families, their personal likes and dislikes, their hobbies and other recreational activities, you'll be able to develop a clearer picture of each individual.

Benefits To Developing This Skill

- You will bring out the best in those with whom you work and play.
- You will create situations that will enable others to achieve success.
- You will develop a better understanding of your impact on others as mentor, supervisor, hard-nose taskmaster, friend and colleague.
- You will be able to bring new hires on line faster, shortening the learning curve.
- Your assessment skills of the performance of others will be honed and judicious.
- Your value to your employer will increase significantly when you can develop the positive characteristics and attributes of others.

Think back to your school days. Was there one teacher, instructor or professor who was able to motivate you to new levels of performance?

Where do people derive the desire to improve themselves? And, what role can you play in facilitating that desire in the workplace and in all areas of your life?

What are the potential pitfalls to taking on the role of inspirational mentor in the workplace, home or social group?

DEVELOPING COMMITMENT IN OTHERS

There's no doubt that to achieve goals, you need commitment and dedication! Anything that requires sustained effort (meeting annual quotas, for example) requires an on-going commitment on the part of your entire team. But how do you nurture this commitment from your teammates?

"When you make a commitment to a relationship, you invest your attention and energy in it more profoundly because you now experience ownership of that relationship." - Barbara De Angelis

There are lots of ways. Recognition of a job well done. Incentives to excel. Using the talents of team members to their best advantage (you wouldn't ask a pitcher in the bullpen to pinch hit, because that not where his talents lie). Perhaps the most important element in creating committed employees is to have clearly stated goals and objectives and to provide regular opportunities for positive reinforcement rather than negative feedback. By creating an environment where achievement is expected, you create an environment in which commitment is a natural outgrowth of your expectations.

"The relationship between commitment and doubt is by no means an antagonistic one. Commitment is healthiest when it's not without doubt but in spite of doubt."

- Rollo May

Benefits To Learning This Skill

- Your team's productivity will increase.
- Your team will be motivated daily to achieve long-term goals.
- You will be the source of commitment on the part of your subordinates and co-workers.
- Your own level of commitment will be raised when you see the same in those with whom you work.
- Your value as a manager/supervisor/team leader will increase, thus making you a more valuable employee to the company.

Unless commitment is made, there are only promises and hopes... but no plans.

- Peter F. Drucker

DISCIPLINARY ACTIVITIES

Perhaps one of the most difficult and unpleasant aspects of serving as a team leader is the need to discipline others - never an easy thing to do. Your approach to this will have an impact on the performance of the individual being disciplined and on the morale of the other team members.

When we review the subject of discipline with managers we look for a process. Has the company implemented an appraisal system? Does the manager perform appraisals in a timely fashion? Has the manager developed goals with the employee and a means of tracking success, or is it all left to chance? Without a system to clearly communicate what is expected, timely follow-up and consistent enforcement of rules and procedures; corporate life can be a bit messy. Developing the ability to correct and offer constructive criticism requires balanced empathy between being too harsh and too easy going. Without the respect of your people and a common vision and mission, you may find this to be a tough job. Remember to divorce yourself of emotion; offer your remarks and look for solutions that benefit all parties, with an eye on what's best for the company.

Some basic guidelines when faced with this task:
- Always remain calm in your discussions.
- Always discipline a team member in private.
- Start by pointing out a positive the individual brings to the table. (You're an excellent sales rep Bob, one of the best I've ever seen.)
- Offer concrete suggestions to improve the performance of the individual.
- Never threaten. It only adds additional pressure on the individual.
- Follow up with positive reinforcement when the employee's performance improves.

POINTS TO PONDER

This is one area where your ability to empathize will come in handy. We've all been disciplined - in school, at work, in public. Before engaging in any disciplinary action, think back to the times you faced disciplinary action. How did you feel afterward?

Also, what steps can you take to make sure your emotions are well in control before taking any disciplinary actions?

THE ETIQUETTE AND RULES OF GOLF

A part of learning to become an emotionally intelligent golfer is the need to follow the rules of the game and the social etiquette upon which the game is based. All-too-often, you observe golfers whose behavior is less than emotionally intelligence. Want some examples?

- Not being ready to play when it's your turn.
- The use of cell phones during the round.
- Not fixing ball marks and divots on the green, fairway or rough.
- Use of unprofessional language.
- Throwing clubs.
- Talking while a player is trying to concentrate.
- Making unwanted noises like jingling coins in the pocket.
- Taking divots on the teeing area during pre-shot routine.
- Taking more than 45 seconds during shot preparation and execution.
- Wearing the wrong apparel for the course environment – tank tops, blue jeans, cut offs, non-collared shirts.

Being a Good Leader

What makes a good leader? Empathy. Compassion. The ability to inspire loyalty from and commitment to the team and to the task. The ability to listen and learn from others - to not believe that you alone have all of the answers.

Effective leadership is putting first things first. Effective management is discipline, carrying it out. - Stephen Covey

---

Good leaders don't need to shout or threaten, they lead by example. They work harder than any other team member, putting in longer hours, shouldering more responsibility, and accepting the consequences of his or her actions on the job.

A good leader protects the other members of the team by running interference for the individual, clearing the decks, setting achievable goals, and using disciplinary actions to teach rather than punish. Leaders are made, not born. More importantly, leaders are made better through experience.

Benefits To Learning This Skill

- You will become more self-reliant.
- You will become more confident in your work skills and your leadership skills.
- You will avoid negative motivators (threats, punishments, penalties, etc.).
- You will focus on what's best for your team, not what's best for you.
- You will be generous with your time and your praise.
- You will defend the members of your team, increasing team loyalty and commitment.
- You will increase your value to the company.

POINTS TO PONDER

Consider some of the great business leaders of today and in the past - people like Jack Welch, ex-CEO of GE, Steve Jobs of Apple, and media favorite, Barbara Walters. Each employs a different approach to leadership. Welch believed strongly in incentives for managers and employees. Jobs create a casual environment in which creative thinking is rewarded. Walters employs a more pro-active management style, insisting on controlling everything from the lighting to the celebrities she interviews.

Obviously, there are many leadership styles, but what common characteristics can you think of that apply to all effective leaders? Bravery? Empathy? The ability to accept failure? Make a list of the characteristics that add up to an effective leader of a business or even a nation.

By letting it go it all gets done. The world is won by those who let it go. But when you try and try, the world is beyond the winning.

- Lao Tzu

Letting Go and learning to give up control of every aspect of every work-related task isn't easy for some, yet delegation of responsibilities is certainly an aspect of good leadership. The good leader knows how to turnover control to others in whom they have confidence, based on past experience.

Your ability to relinquish control to others accomplishes several key things:
- It frees up your time and energy for other matters.
- It shows that you have confidence in the other members of your team.
- It increases commitment on the part of all stakeholders.
- It adds new thinking and ideas to any long-term project.

POINTS TO PONDER

You reluctantly assign a crucial project to a member of your team - a project that will ultimately have your name on it, as in you're responsible.

As the project gets underway, you monitor it very closely for the first few weeks, but then, as your confidence in the assigned team member grows, you're able to walk away a bit - to remove yourself from the day-to-day worries.

What are the pros and cons to relinquishing control, even to a trusted team member? What advantages are there to the individual team member, the team as a whole and to you, the team leader? And, how can assigning an important project to a co-worker blow up in your face?

RELATING TO OTHERS

This may sound like a no-brainer, but it's not. In fact, your ability to relate to others on both a professional and personal level is, in large measure, what the development of EQ is all about.

In the workplace, you have people who manage your activities and in turn, you manage the activities of others. How you relate to these different co-workers will often determine your ultimate success on the job.

Relating to others involves the development of an important ability - the ability to develop insight into the personalities of others - the things that motivate them, frighten them, and make them happy or depressed. It involves your ability to 'read' the feelings of others at a specific time and over the course of time. In fact, relating to others involves almost all of the attributes we've introduced in this chapter.

Remember, EQ is intended to make you a happier, healthier person internally - an individual with increased confidence and good judgment, empathy and understanding of what motivates you and the people around you. In fact, your social skills are the outward manifestation of your social awareness - your awareness of the feelings of others and adapting to those feelings to improve whatever situation you find yourself in.

It's not a one-time learning experience. It's an on-going process, one that never ends. You will continue to develop EQ proficiencies within the seven dimensions of emotional intelligence and you, and the rest of the world around you, will be better for the effort.

Benefits To Learning This Skill

- You will be a better leader.
- You will be a stronger team player.
- You will be a better spouse, friend, co-worker, supervisor, and human being.
- Your awareness of your effect on others will be enhanced and improved.
- You will always be improving; you will never stop learning.
- You will have stronger, more fulfilling relationships in virtually every area of your life.

POINTS TO PONDER

Because humans, by nature, are social animals, personal interactions are not only important, they help us define who we are to ourselves and others. What is your strongest interpersonal attribute? Are you a natural-born leader? A teacher? Mentor? Motivator? When dealing with others at work, and in the other areas of your life, what is your strongest personal asset?

Conversely, what attribute do you feel needs attention? Are you impatient?

Distant and aloof? Unwilling to take risks, or too willing to take risks? Find a quiet moment to reflect on your relationships with others and how these relationships can be improved by maximizing your interpersonal strengths while mitigating the impact of your shortcomings on yourself and on others.

HIGHER LEVEL THINKING AND SITUATIONAL INTELLIGENCE™

CHAPTER ELEVEN | Congratulations!

You've come a great distance on you journey to self-improvement. You've discovered the seven dimensions of emotional intelligence and dozens of skills associated with these dimensions.

You've learned to be a better listener. Perhaps you've developed empathy for a co-worker. Or, perhaps you've identified a few areas within yourself that you'd like to change and improve.

You have changed from reading this book, even if you don't agree with every point (which is fine, it shows you're thinking for yourself). You've changed because, by reading this book, you have heightened awareness of EQ and the role it plays in your contentment and the happiness and well-being of those with whom you live, work and play. That, in itself, is a marvelous achievement - one that you will carry with you long after you've put this book down.

Your vision will become clear only when you can look into your own heart .
Who looks outside, dreams; who looks inside, awakes.   - Carl G. Jung

Indeed, you have come far on your road to self-discovery. Now, how do you put this new knowledge to work in the real world? In the next two chapters, you'll learn how the seven dimensions of emotional intelligence, and the attendant skills associated with each of these dimensions, can dovetail to create the better employee, spouse, golfer, parent and human being you want to become. It's not enough to heighten awareness of EQ. This increased awareness must be put to practical use in the everyday world to have true significance in your life and the lives of others.

Your heightened awareness of the concept of EQ, and your on-going, conscious effort to apply the principles that underlie the concept, will be put to use in a number of internal (self-improvement) ways and external (interaction with others) ways. These proficiencies will better equip you for higher-level thinking - outside the box thinking - that will be used in virtually every endeavor you undertake.

So, let's look at the next step of your journey - the use of higher levels of EQ to achieve higher levels of thinking. Specifically, let's examine the thinking skills associated with:

- Integrative abilities.
- Intuitive decision making.
- Problem and situational analysis.
- Problem management.
- Theoretical problem solving.
- Systems judgment.

If some of these abilities are unfamiliar to you, don't worry. These are activities that are a part of your life every day. Now, we'll examine how your developing EQ can be used to perform these daily tasks efficiently, effectively, and with confidence.

Integrative Activates

We don't exist in a vacuum. We are connected to the people in our lives, the things in our lives and the activities that take place within our lives. For example, you interact with family and co-workers, people on the street, friends, and total strangers. You also interact with things - your car, your home, the bicycle you bought with 'some assembly required' - the physical world is our environment and we all interact with it.

Finally, you interact with the systems that are such a part of our lives. These include the system of laws under which we act, the office rules, manners, customs and traditions - these aren't physical aspects of your life, nonetheless, they are an essential ingredient of life - and one in which emotional intelligence plays a significant role.

With all of these interactions taking place, problems will arise. Those with little or no concept of self-awareness and the inability to feel empathy might be inclined to commit a crime since they lack the ability to feel what the victim of a crime would feel. Or, perhaps the individual who lacks self-management proficiencies, coupled with under-developed communication skills, might not be the best choice for the development of the quarterly report due next week.

The ability to integrate the internal, external and systems attributes to make the best use of available resources is a highly-valued skill, and one requiring high levels of EQ. Individuals with the ability to integrate people (and their activities), the physical world (office, golf course) and the systems that direct human behavior (laws, rules, protocols, procedures) are 'big picture' thinkers.

Individuals who have developed integrative abilities are proficient leaders, maximizing individual and group potential. They are adept at assigning the right tasks to the right individuals - the ones who can get the job done, and done properly.

People with strong integrative abilities are strong leaders - strong because they have the vision and self-management skills to keep their focus on the finish, and strong because they're able to work with others in a supportive, empathetic manner. They don't bully and bluster; they lead by example. The result is a loyal team, willing and eager to do what it takes to get the job done - for their team leader.

Integrative skills involve one's ability to assess the personal, the environmental and the system integration in all the aspects of workplace activity - not only the best person for the job, but using the appropriate motivator for the employee and the task at hand.

People with strong integrative skills have high levels of emotional intelligence and make the best supervisors and managers.

These men and women:

- Make maximum use of resources to create synergy (1 + 1 = 3).
- Respect and adhere to the protocols, rules, laws, customs, etc. (aka systems).
- Are able to understand others, their feelings, their motivations, their self-image, their strengths and limitations. This assessment ability enables these leaders to maximize strengths and mitigate limitations.
- Can see, not only the end result, but also the processes required to achieve the end result. They have strong organizational, conceptual, and analytic skills.
- Bring out the best in people with whom they work and live. They make lives better for those around them.
- Are not only team leaders, they feel they are also members of the team. The need to belong is strong within individuals with integrative skills.
- Seek to bring order to chaos. In the middle of a big project, they're the ones who can answer the questions and keep many things moving simultaneously.
- Enjoy their successes and share each success with every team member.
- Are highly goal oriented (goal achievement is a strong motivator).
- Continue to develop and grow their self-esteem and self-image from their leadership roles.
- Have an understanding of their needs and drives (self-awareness).
- Are dedicated to whatever tasks they undertake. (self-management).
- Are willing to accept challenges and think 'outside-the-box' for solutions.

- View co-workers, the work place, and the systems in place, as an integrated whole.
- Are confident in their decisions and keep moving forward despite setbacks.

Increased EQ equips you to maximize your strengths while diminishing the effect of limitations on your personal and professional lives.

INTUITIVE DECISION MAKING
"IT'S JUST A GUT FEELING I HAVE."

" You'll be flying by the seat of your pants on this one."

"I have a sixth sense about these things.""In a moment of clarity you just know."

The human brain is a wonderful machine. It can store huge amounts of data and retrieve it in a split second, it can manipulate abstract concepts and arrive at a completely new concept, it has the ability to judge and assess, calculate and plan, see into the future to project outcomes - and, even so, the entire scientific community is just beginning to understand how some of these brain functions operate.

There are theories and postulates, but no concrete, scientific evidence to tell us how the brain functions. Why do twins score higher on mental telepathy assessments? We have the data to show it's true, but all we have is anecdotal evidence. No science.

Intuition falls into this group of brain function unknowns. There's plenty of anecdotal evidence that intuition exists, but how can we prove it? Well, for many of us, no proof is required. We've experienced intuition many times before, and when we "go with our gut feelings" things usually turn out just fine. So, is it some mystical power that only some people possess? Is it up there with ESP, telekinesis and remote viewing? Well possibly. While no one can be certain, there are some reasonable assumptions that can be made about our ability to intuit.

As we age, we accumulate more and more knowledge. Born the well-known 'blank slate', we learn throughout our lives - everything from our ABCs to how to decode the human genome. The conscious accumulates data in several ways. First, by conscious effort. These are the things we learn in a formal setting - formal learning - things like the multiplication tables or advanced calculus, the proper use of language and the traditions and customs, sometimes called the lore, that forms the underpinnings of our culture and society.

Experiential learning is just that - learning from experience. You can tell a child not to touch, "Hot! Hot! Don't touch!" a million times and the child won't learn the lesson. However, one touch and a 'boo-boo' on the finger usually gets the point across.

Much experiential learning is empirical learning - learning done through your own five senses - sight, hearing, taste, touch, and smell. You learn that snow is cold by feeling it. You learn that roses smell wonderful by smelling one. You learn you may not like spinach by tasting it. Empirical learning is the accumulation of knowledge gathered by us directly through one or more of the five senses. We learn directly, without an intermediary, such as a teacher or mentor. Experiential learning occurs at both the conscious and subconscious level.

In addition to formal learning and experiential learning, there's also sub-conscious learning - learning that takes place without you even being aware it's occurred. The sub-conscious collects real-world data every day.

There's a well-known example of sub-conscious learning told in many psychology classes because it makes the point so well. A woman was sleeping when she had a terrible dream. She dreamt that she was standing on her apartment balcony and fell off when the wrought-iron railing gave way. The dream was so real, so upsetting, that the woman went straight to the balcony, jiggled the railing and, sure enough, it was loose.

At some previous point, the woman's sub-conscious noticed a slight wiggle in the railing, something the woman's conscious missed because, perhaps she was on the telephone or just thinking of something else. In any case, the subconscious picked up this important information and delivered it to the conscious by way of a dream. Keep this in mind as we talk a bit about intuition.

The fact is, you don't know what you know. That's right. Don't you amaze yourself sometimes when you can recall the name of your first grade teacher decades later? Are you ever pleasantly surprised when you're the only one who can find a viable solution to a job problem? Do your instincts always seem to point you down the right path? Amazing, isn't it?

Well, not really. Intuition is the ability to use formal, experiential and sub-conscious learning to make choices and decisions. In many cases, you "just can't put your finger" on why you should do something, but you know you should. But there's really nothing mystical about it.

Intuitive decision-making is something we all do everyday, without thought. It's a skill, an attribute - something upon which you can improve. A heightened awareness of the feelings of others, greater confidence in yourself, an improved ability to communicate effectively - these are all the result of heightened EQ, and, coincidentally, all associated with the workings of human intuition.

When faced with a problem, the brain goes to work to find a solution. In doing so, your brain calls upon your formal learning, experiential learning, and your sub-conscious learning to arrive at a workable solution. You bring to bear an array of thinking tools - some of which you don't even know you possess - when seeking the solution to a problem, or weighing the consequences of one choice over another. Intuitive decision-making happens daily in the workplace.

You might not be able to put all of the pieces together. You might not know, for certain, the final outcome. You're aware that your decision may be wrong - but you make it anyway, with confidence, because your instincts tell you to. Your instincts are based on many factors - experiences, problem-solving skills, formal education, sub-conscious learning, motivations and drives - the brain, that magnificent machine, is capable of taking all of these aspects of thinking to arrive at a decision based on intuition.

People with high levels of intuition also possess high levels of emotional awareness and sensitivity to the environment. People with good instincts:

- Have strong problem-solving skills.
- Are driven by results.
- Are sensitive to the feelings and thoughts of others.
- Possess good 'common sense'.

- Are able to evaluate and assess consequences to choices and decisions.
- Have high levels of self-confidence based on positive past experiences.
- Are confident in their positions in the workplace (role awareness).
- Tend to be practical, down-to-earth thinkers rather than mystical diviners of the future.
- Are self-motivated, self-managed and 'outside-the-box' thinkers.

People who have intuitive decision-making skills are valuable employees. They're leaders and free thinkers, problem-solvers and achievers. On the other hand, there are people who place too much stock in their intuition. These people tend to ignore the thoughts and feelings of others, miss the small details along the way, and hope to get lucky.

When used judiciously and intelligently, intuitive decision-making is a valuable asset. It should be an element in the weighting process that occurs as we mull over a problem and various solutions or options. However, it should be used in conjunction with both our formal and experiential learning to arrive at the best decision most often.

PROBLEM/SITUATIONAL ANALYSIS

Each day you're faced with problems that need to be solved and situations that need to be handled. It's an aspect of work; an aspect of life. But, it's just as true that some people are able to solve problems and manage situations better than others, a function of their higher levels of emotional intelligence.

Individuals with the ability to analyze a problem tend to see the problem and it's many facets, e.g. the source of the problem, the nature of the problem, the effects of the problem, and so on. And, through their ability to take a multi-dimensional view of the problem, these are the problem-solvers among us.

People with strong problem and situational analysis skills gather as much factual and perceptual information as possible. Factual information would include things like numbers, past performance, available resources, deadlines and so on. Perceptual information includes people's feelings about a problem, their opinions, their proposed solutions and the impact the problem has on their lives.

This factual and perceptual information is then taken apart and put back together again. Interconnections are changed, the shape of the problem is more clearly defined and solutions start to present themselves. Maybe not the solutions, but the process has begun.

It may take time. Additional information may be required to accurately analyze a problem. All of the pieces might not be there, but as you mull things over, a course of action begins to emerge. With additional information (and more mulling), people with an aptitude for problem analysis will arrive at a well-considered conclusion and a solution to the problem will be implemented.

People with this skill are also able to identify problems early, before that little problem becomes a full-blown catastrophe. Because of this ability to catch a problem before it gets out of hand, people with situational analysis skills make excellent employees, recognized for their value to the company.

People who are able to analyze a problem or a given set of circumstances (a situation) possess high levels of EQ and have mastered many of the proficiencies associated with the dimensions of EQ.

People with this skill:

- Possess a positive attitude about problems, viewing them as challenges rather than problems.
- Identify problems in their infancy.
- See the whole problem with its many facets. They are able to conceptualize the problem and manipulate its various aspects.
- Are able to remain calm under pressure (self-management) allowing their thought processes to continue even with external stress.
- Are able to sort through the facts and determine the relevance of each to the problem and ultimate solution.
- Actively solicit the input and opinions of others. These people are confident in their own skills and decision-making processes so that they can listen to the ideas and opinions of others without feeling threatened.
- Attempt to develop more than one solution to a problem, then weigh the different solutions to select the best.
- Accept responsibility for their decisions, good, bad, or indifferent.

- Are able to break down large problems into constituent parts, which can then be analyzed individually to better understand their place in the larger problem.
- Seek the approval of other stakeholders before implementing a solution to a problem.

One possible downside to individuals with this valuable skill is affixed in the social domain. These analytical thinkers are often 'results orientated' to the exclusion of the thoughts and feelings of others, they often act without weighing the personal consequences and, in some instances, the problem becomes all-consuming to the point where the individual can no longer function in their other capacities, i.e., bringing the problem home with them, thus throwing their work-life balance out of whack.

PROBLEM MANAGEMENT

Associated with problem/situational analysis, problem management also involves analytical skills and a strong sense of who's best suited to do the best job. Problem analysis involves breaking down a problem into smaller pieces, then finding solutions to the little problems that comprise the big problem. Problem management measures an individual's ability to handle numerous problems while 'keeping the lid on' and preventing things from boiling over.

The skills associated with problem management fall into the dimensions of emotional intelligence and their associated proficiencies. For example, as a manager, you're in the best position to delegate responsibility to the members of the team best suited to handle each task. This comes from developing an understanding of the strengths and limitations of team members, but it also involves such things as the ability to work under stress, the ability to analyze, collate, and communicate effectively.

Prioritization is another aspect of problem management with a direct correlation to EQ proficiencies. The ability to rank work-related tasks by priority requires excellent work assessment skills, problem solving-skills, team unity, personnel management and a strong bond between team leader and team members.

Finally, the ability to manage problems in the workplace invariably requires the ability to remain calm under pressure and the ability to self-manage, that is, keep focused on the tasks, keep those balls in the air and look forward to the time when things slow down.

People with high levels of EQ view problems as opportunities to affect change and implement improvements. For example, while attempting to gather and collate monthly departmental data, you may suddenly realize that procedures could be streamlined if persons A and B worked in tandem rather than at two different stages of a given process. While not earth shattering, it's the kind of thing that happens every day as you manage the different problems that cross your desk. In fact, that's one of the primary attributes of a good leader.

People with the ability to manage a myriad of problems successfully and calmly:

- Let others know what is expected of them.
- Have strong problem/situational analysis skills.
- Understand the personal motivators of team members.
- Are driven to achieve the desired result when confronted with a set of problems.
- Are able to bring out the best in other team members.
- Share the spotlight, or better still, shine the spotlight on individual team members.
- Set realistic goals for the team and for themselves.
- Have excellent long-range, problem-solving skills.
- Are able to keep focus under pressure.
- Can correct the activities of others with sensitivity, not to chastise, but to improve individual performance.
- Are confident in the managerial skills and decision-making processes.
- Believe strongly in the work ethic for themselves and others.

The problems associated with these team leaders are, again, related to personal interactions. These multi-taskers are sometimes so focused on the development of solutions that they overlook the feelings, thoughts, and opinions of others. They may tend to take on too much responsibility, believing that only they can get the tasks completed in a timely manner. Finally, people with high levels of problem management skills often apply the same skills to interpersonal relationships. Rather than building strong, mutually beneficial relationships, people in the business of problem management often view co-workers as resources and assets (or liabilities) rather than individuals with needs, desires, and drives.

THEORETICAL PROBLEM SOLVING

The development of situational intelligence requires the development of theoretical problem solving skills, though the two might seem antithetical. Situational intelligence involves the here and now - the systems in place, the resources available, and the task at hand. It's practical, applied, and an essential part of the good supervisor's day. It's nuts and bolts thinking, but in fact, the ability to handle life's boilerplate effectively and efficiently is, in fact, an abstract skill that's applied in our three-dimensional, physical world.

Theoretical problem solving takes you into the realm of 'what ifs' and here, the rules are very different from the gravity-ladened world in which we live. You're dealing with abstract concepts the way a chess master moves pieces on a chessboard. And there's no doubt, that this qualifies as a higher level of thinking, one that requires many of the attributes associated with emotional intelligence: problem management, persistence, quality orientation, sensitivity to others - as you're mentally manipulating the elements of the problem, you're using all of these attributes and many others associated with high degrees of emotional intelligence. Now, as you're manipulating these abstractions, you're not conscious of these attributes of EQ at work in your search for a solution. These attributes are a part of your character, so ingrained that they require little or no thought.

People with a strong aptitude for theoretical problem solving:
- Are able to manipulate abstract concepts and predict the outcome of each manipulation with a substantial degree of certainty.
- Are able to view the entire scope of the problem, both short- and long-term, and develop intermediate solutions when called for.

- Have vivid imaginations.
- Enjoy a challenge and may even view challenges as puzzles, something fun to solve.
- Consider the human element in their hypothetical evaluations.
- Have highly developed conceptual skills and an ability to combine resources in new ways to produce a more efficient, productive operation or process.
- Are less result oriented, placing a greater emphasis on developing the process.
- Are highly creative in other areas of their lives.
- Are inclined to develop proactive rather than reactive solutions based on the theoretical nature of the problem under consideration.
- Are self-directed, requiring very little oversight. They are independent thinkers, even intellectual pioneers in the button down world of corporate America. But they're the ones who start it all.

Those with highly developed theoretical problem solving skills usually have emotional intelligence attributes that might be seen as underdeveloped, though certainly not in every case. These thinkers often neglect the feelings of others. They become engrossed in the problem and may even miss a birthday or some other important event - the classic absent-minded professor - but there's more than a grain of truth to the stereotype.

So, you might see underdeveloped social skills or self-management skills. You might even see an inflated ego or two when you examine these thinkers of deep thoughts. They're systems analysts, computer coders, efficiency consultants, productivity consultants - men and women who spend a good part of their workdays in the world of abstractions and ideations.

SYSTEMS JUDGMENT

As we mentioned previously, we live in a world of interlocking and cross-connecting systems. Some of the more influential systems in our daily lives include:

- Local, state and federal laws.
- Office rules and regulations.

- Work-related operations and procedures.
- 'Civilized' behavior which includes good manners (Mom was right!) and cordiality to all.
- School, association or affiliation rules and regulations.
- Social customs such as holding the door open for someone behind you
- Traditions - everything from graduations to weddings to funerals

These are just some of the systems in our lives, providing guidance in proper behavior. Then, when you factor in house rules, the sacred rules of your lodge, the laws of physics, and all of the other systems that are a part of our daily lives, it becomes easier to recognize the importance of systems judgment.

For example, your ability to evaluate the in-place reporting procedures from your field reps and develop a streamlined process that provides more information faster and with less time on the part of the reps, is a gift. Everybody wins - and you made it happen! The fact is, systems judgment involves systems analysis to arrive at your assessment, your judgment.

This most valuable skill is a key aspect of higher levels of EQ, and a skill that can be developed through your heightened awareness of the proficiencies associated with sound systems judgment. People with this skill:

- Are able to grasp the big picture and the minute details.
- Are results driven, always trying to improve results.
- Are highly efficient and value efficiency in others.
- Recognize their own place within these diverse systems.
- Have a strong belief in the importance of concrete systems, procedures and protocols.
- Have a very strong ability to remember and utilize small details.
- Appreciate the rewards of a job well done.

However, as with all of these higher-thinking capabilities, people with strong abilities to assess, judge and adjust systems often focus on the system and not the people affected by the system. They may often score low on the dimensions of social skills and social awareness. They see things as either black or white. Either it works or it doesn't. Next!

They're motivated by success, which may come at the expense of people's jobs. Improving operations is the ultimate goal.

Improved skills in integrative ability, intuitive decision making, problem and situational analysis, problem management, theoretical problem solving and systems judgment are the natural result of heightened awareness of the seven dimensions of emotional intelligence and the skills associated with each dimension.

These are the attributes of people who have made the conscious decision to make themselves better managers, better employees, better spouses, better parents, better human beings. Sure, you may score off the chart on self-management skills and still lack self- discipline, always waiting to get the job done just before it's due. We all have strengths and weakness. Any strength carried to an extreme can become a weakness. It is because we are multi-faceted creatures that nature helps to balance out our strengths and weaknesses. Even Mary Poppins wasn't perfect, though she was almost perfect in everyway.

HIGH LEVEL THINKING ON THE COURSE

"Aim for mastery in learning. The masters are those who have achieved great skill, ease and versatility at what they do. When we think of mastery, we usually imagine artisans, musicians or artists who have worked for decades, but mastery can be achieved in any task right from the first tiny step." - Michael Hebron,
The Zen and Art of Learning Golf

Before we can reach the stage of high-level thinking and development, human beings need to create a balance between their mental, emotional and physical aspects of self. When this balance occurs, the person becomes an integrated, mature ego.

Becoming a truly mature ego, requires on-going training and mastery in many different areas of personal development. Studies have shown that achieving this level of maturity does not occur automatically. Only on-going, long-term training will do this.

This is why emotional intelligence, for example, cannot be learned and mastered in a seminar or workshop. But rather, the personal and social skill sets of emotional intelligence need to be applied first in role-play and practical exercises such as golf (or other sports) and business, and then in the real world. For this to occur, companies will hire EQ coaches who can provide both the business and sports applications so that the long-term development of their employees can occur.

Integration requires a person to integrate and balance the many parts, which make us whole as a human person. The lessons we are learning by understanding and applying the emotional intelligence competencies in our daily lives show us where we stand today, and the work we still need to do for future development.

Top thinkers in the human evolutionary movement are talking about integration, and the need for all people to create their own integral training and development programs. Some of the top thinkers in the integral movement are Stanislav Grof, Fred Kofman, Jack Kornfield, George Leonard, Michael Murphy, Jenny Wade, Roger Walsh, Ken Wilber, Peggy Wright, and Michael Zimmerman. The integral movement includes the areas of business, education, medicine, psychology, politics, spirituality and sports.

Golf Inside & Out has created an integrated curriculum for golfers. By applying the skills sets found in each quadrant and stage of development, the golfer can integrate their human development, while at the same time, they can grow in their abilities for mastering the game. Another golf company that has been on the cutting edge of integral golf training is Vision 54 – Coaching for the Future, owned by Pia Nilsson and Lynn Marriott.   *- David Geier, CEO*
Golf Inside & Out

BEGINNING THE INTEGRAL JOURNEY IN GOLF

For most players, the quest for consistency in golf begins with the improvement of their swing mechanics or technical skills. This journey begins in the physical dimension of development and is a correct and proper starting point for golfers wanting to play the game. However, this would also be a limited, one-dimensional approach, if any of the equally important developmental components found with the physical dimension are not taken into consideration, e.g. fitness, diet, equipment, emotional and mental states, self-awareness, behavioral styles, and witness consciousness.

From a holistic perspective, this means that a golfer would select two, three, or more items within the physical dimension and practice them concurrently. This begins to create a balanced approach for enhancing physical capabilities. This beginning stage will become the foundation for the higher and more advanced stages of development found in the emotional, mental, transpersonal, and spiritual stages.

As golfers progress in their integral training, they will include other practices, such as emotional intelligence training, which will help raise their level of development and consciousness into the higher realms of thinking and being.

In addition to these aspects of higher thinking, your heightened levels of EQ will also improve the practical side of your work and personal life, making you a better (no, a great) team player, learning to give up the reins once in a while, and accepting the consequences of your actions without flinching.

So let's look at other benefits you'll derive as you continue to develop even higher levels of EQ; Becoming a Great Playing Partner as discussed in Chapter 12.

BECOMING A GREAT
PLAYING PARTNER

CHAPTER TWELVE | There's a fundamental dichot-
omy in human nature. At once, we look out for our own best interests,
being anything but a great team player, and simultaneously, we give of
ourselves for the greater good of the team. Think about it. There are times
in all of our lives when we've been selfish, uncooperative, stubborn and
petty. There have also been times when we've been compassionate and
empathetic, making personal sacrifices for the good of the team, be it our
family team, workplace team, or 'taking one' for your baseball team. Our
need to belong is side by side with our need for self-preservation, causing
conflicts that might be called 'moral dilemmas'.

*"A mind once stretched by a great idea or new understanding,
will never fully return to its' original dimensions."* - *Williams James*

The benefit to developing higher levels of emotional intelligence, and
the skills associated with the dimensions of EQ, is an improved team

player - an individual who makes life better for them self and those in their sphere. Good team players cooperate, share the load and lift up a teammate when falling short. As a team, we can accomplish more in less time, much like the old barn raisings when the entire community turned out to erect a barn and eat homemade cooking set out by the womenfolk. It would take one guy six weeks to get the barn up. It takes the team of barn-raisers a day to accomplish the same amount of work. Teamwork gets the job done.

But teams need leaders as well as followers. Leaders determine the direction the team will take and the strategy for success. They oversee the activities of individual team members to determine that all is functioning as it should. There needs to be a 'captain', a 'foreman', a 'director', or 'CEO' - an individual (or individuals) who help the members of the team improve their skills, who keep the team cohesive, who takes responsibility, and delegates authority. Whether we're talking about a group of volunteers erecting a new playground in town, or the President of a Fortune 500 company, every team needs a leader or leaders.

Now, as you might expect, a team directed by a leader with higher levels of EQ is more likely to perform at optimum levels than a team directed by a leader with fewer skills (proficiencies) associated with EQ. For example, a good leader, one with a well-developed EQ, will listen to the advice of others without feeling threatened. The less qualified leader, at least in terms of EQ, is likely to see advice from others as a threat to his or her position as leader and, thus, is born the tyrant, the dictator, the office emperor.

So, let's examine how an increased awareness of EQ and EQ-associated skills will turn you into a more effective leader when it's your turn to call the shots.

"The most satisfying thing in life is to have been able to give a large part of one's self to others." - Pierre Teilhard de Chardin

Developing Others

Developing the strengths of others is a critical leadership function for the simple reason that as the skills of individuals improve, the stronger the team becomes. A chain is only as strong as its weakest link. Learning to develop skills in others requires an understanding of individual needs and motivations, areas of strength, and areas that are underdeveloped, and the ability to use this information to best effect.

As a teacher, mentor or coach, it's important that the teacher-student relationship be one based on trust - trust that the teacher will be patient and nurturing, and the trust that the student is willing, even eager, to learn.

At times, you will be the teacher, while at other times, perhaps under different circumstances, you'll be the student. Individuals with high levels of EQ are, indeed, eager to learn. And through learning, the entire team becomes stronger.

However, it's important to note the distinction between mentor or teacher and director or 'boss'. Part of developing EQ skills is developing the ability to facilitate the activities of others without actually directing them. People learn at their own pace and in their own ways. We learn from our successes, but we learn even more from our failures. Be proactive, stay involved, be available for consultation, but don't direct the activities of your 'students'.

The skills, attitudes and activities required of any good teacher are all associated with emotional intelligence:

- You must be willing to put in the time and energy to teach or coach. Your day may be filled from sun up to sundown, but to develop others, you have to make time in your busy day to serve as a mentor or teacher. Further, you must make it known that you're available throughout the day. Make time; make yourself available.
- You should place a high value on your responsibility and opportunity to develop others. However, know when to back away and give up control.
- As a mentor, teacher, instructor, or supervisor, patience is, indeed, a virtue. Without patience, your students won't approach you as readily, diminishing your value as an instructor and 'enlightened leader'.

- Make it known that you will hold each student (or subordinate) responsible for their workplace performance. Yes, you should be patient, but you're also the one who sets the bar. If you set high standards and hold people accountable for meeting those standards, you've provided the students with their objective and empowered them to achieve their own success.

Finally, with an increased awareness of the needs and drives of others, and an increased awareness of each individual team member's learning style, pace, motivation, and so on, you should be flexible in your teaching methodologies. For example, some people see things more clearly when the information is presented visually. So, draw a blueprint or make a chart. Adapt your approach to teaching or mentoring to suit the student's strengths and weaknesses; and remember adults learn by doing.

"There's so much spontaneity involved, what do you practice? How do you practice teamwork? How do you practice sharing? How do you practice daring? How do you practice being nonjudgmental?"

- Herbie Hancock

Fostering Teamwork: Relating to Others

A team is a group of people who share relationships. Thus, building solid, healthy relationships with others is key to fostering teamwork.

You hear a lot about people skills or "she's a people person". The reason is simple: your ability to develop positive relationships in your life will be a big factor in just how satisfying and fulfilling that life is. But good, strong bonds don't just happen. You have to make them happen. It requires a conscious effort on your part to create the kind of relationships that make any team stronger.

Relating to others doesn't mean you have to get all touchy/feely, but it does require some basic skills, and perhaps an attitude readjustment here and there, but it's all part of the learning and growing experience that comes with higher levels of EQ.

RELATING TO OTHERS:

- Start by recognizing and respecting the value of each individual - even the co-worker whose suit is always covered with cat hair. This is especially important in the workplace where a diverse group of individual personalities and values works as a team, with varying degrees of success.

- Be the calm one. When word comes down from on high (the CEO's office) that "the crunch is on," keep your composure. It's an attribute of a good team leader.

- In the workplace, don't just develop horizontal relationships, develop vertical relationships, as well. Work to establish a trusting relationship with your manager and their manager as well as the people who report to you. These are vertical relationships, running from Lenny in the mailroom to the levels of management above you.

- Evaluate people by performance, not by your own, subjective criteria. Whether or not the guy in the last cubicle graduated from college is utterly irrelevant when you know he's the only one who can fix the copy machine. You can't judge people based on your biases. Each individual should be evaluated on performance.

- Listen and learn. Recognize that your ideas aren't always the best ideas. Listen to others and go with the best ideas. People will be more inclined to approach you if they know you're receptive to new ideas.

ACCEPTING RESPONSIBILITY

Being in a leadership role requires accountability - the accountability of each team member to you and, of course, your accountability to upper-level managers. It comes with the territory. In the working world, the buck stops with you - the manager of the activities of others.

Establishing a system of accountability requires a number of skills - organizational skills, problem-solving skills, teaching/mentoring skills, evaluation skills and others, as well. You must be able to accurately assess the capabilities of those working under you and delegate accordingly, assigning the right person to the right job.

You must also be able to improve the performance of employees by correcting under-productive or counterproductive behavior and activity. You must keep up team morale and build-in opportunities for success. Success is a great motivator and once people have experienced it, they want to experience it again.

One important part of your role as manager is to make your expectations known - that you will hold others accountable for their work, rewarding good work while correcting sub-par performance.

Set goals - individual and departmental goals. The goals should be realistic and, of course, achievable. When goals are met, be generous with your praise and always give credit where credit is due. Never take credit for the work of others. It will severely diminish your capacity to lead, and it's ethically wrong.

There's an old saying: It takes 30 days to break a habit and 30 days to start one. If bad habits are already in place, be patient as you correct them and institute new policies, procedures, and protocols. At first, some employees will resist or be reluctant to go along with the new reforms, but in time, if done with empathy and patience, in a few short months you'll be able to increase individual and team productivity, maintain a happier group of employees who know what's expected of them and, you'll have the personal satisfaction that comes with the design and implementation of a successful plan.

The skills, activities and attitudes associated with your ability to both delegate and accept responsibility come directly as a result of your increased awareness of EQ:

- Set the standards for those who work under you and maintain the same set of standards for yourself. If members of the team are required to work through a weekend, be there with them. That's being accountable.

- When delegating responsibility, make sure that you also provide the resources required to meet the responsibility. Resources might include additional manpower, a reasonable delivery schedule, new equipment, additional training, and so on. To assign a task, and then not provide the means necessary to complete the task successfully is not good for team morale.

- Make corrections when necessary. Though you may not like to address the weaknesses of others, you may have to in your position as manager. If you identify a shortcoming, bring it to the employee's attention quickly, but also with sensitivity. The overbearing bully approach does little for morale or for your image of an approachable resource.

- Identify systems problems rather than problems caused by individual employees. For example, when the department falls short of its quarterly numbers, don't point the finger at the lowest producer. Instead, identify where, in the system, changes could be made to improve the performance of all producers. This takes the analysis out of the realm of the personal and keeps focus on improvement, not blame.

- Encourage creative problem solving. As manager, you may not be in the best position to identify small areas where improvements can be implemented. Listen to employees and encourage their input with regard to departmental activities.

- Be generous with your praise and let the other members of the team see this. Make announcements of outstanding performance or unusual initiative. Don't be afraid to share the spotlight. It's what good managers do.

- Criticize quietly. Just as you want others to hear your praise, keep your criticisms quiet and private. Never publicly chastise an employee. It's counterproductive. It lowers morale and identifies you as someone who can't be trusted. Remember, good business relationships are based on trust.

"Most folks are about as happy as they make up their minds to be."

- Abraham Lincoln

WHAT ARE YOU DOING? - ROLE AWARENESS

We've all met people who go through life leaving a trail of carnage behind them. They cut in line, oblivious to the icy stares of others. They say rude things, or do hurtful things, completely unaware that they've hurt the feelings of others. In many cases, these people are simply so self-absorbed that they just don't care about others. In all cases, these people lack any kind of role awareness.

Role awareness is simply being aware of what you're supposed to be doing, what you are doing, how you're doing it, and the impact these things have on your co-workers. Got that?

We play a variety of roles in our lives - parent or child, employee, manager, coach, citizen and so on, and as we assume each one of these roles, we must be aware of who we are and what we're doing. It may sound obvious, but to the guy who stole your parking space at the store last week, it's anything but obvious.

Being aware of your role within a given environment - the workplace, for example - involves an understanding of your place in the pecking order, an understanding of your responsibilities and the responsibilities of those above and below you within that pecking order.

Role awareness also requires an understanding of expectations - the expectations of those you manage and the expectations of those who manage you. In other words, what are you doing?

Can you think back to your first day on the job? You didn't know anyone, you weren't sure what your responsibilities were, and you didn't even know whom to ask! So you fumbled your way through that first day trying to look busy while remaining clueless as to just what you were supposed to be doing and how to do it. But as the days, weeks and months passed, you developed role awareness - your understanding of who you were in the organization and what was expected of you. On the first day, your desk was empty because no one had any expectations of you - yet. Today, you can't even see the top of your desk because everyone has expectations of you - quotas to meet, deadlines to hit, reports to complete. No doubt, after a few months, you were well aware of your role within the company.

Unfortunately, some people never develop role awareness. They never develop a sense of purpose or even a reason to show up at work every day. People like these are reactive, reacting to events happening around them.

Those with higher levels of role awareness tend to be proactive because they know what's expected and they know how to complete the mission.

Further, those with role awareness are more productive because they keep the objective in sight and they develop a strategy to reach that objective. Those with lower levels of role awareness may never see the big picture. They'll make false starts, hesitate and backtrack, always second guessing themselves. A clear picture of your role within the company - your responsibilities, expectations and the expectations of others - is a critical factor in workplace success.

The skills, attitudes and activities associated with role awareness are, somewhat, intuitive, though they can be learned as you develop higher levels of EQ:

- Role awareness assumes that you know your job. You've set down your expectations of those you manage and have a clear understanding of what's expected of you.

- Role awareness also involves your ability to make decisions. If you're confident in your role, you'll naturally make confident decisions - the tough decisions required of a business leader in today's competitive economy. You'll also stop second-guessing your decisions, a totally counter-productive activity.

- Being aware of your role enables you to ask for clarification without fear of 'looking stupid'. Your supervisor gives your department an assignment, along with a lengthy, detailed set of steps to be followed. Secure in your role as the one responsible for completing this assignment successfully, you can confidently ask for clarifications from your supervisor and others with no fear of looking stupid.

- Not all expectations are spelled out. With increased role awareness, you'll understand the well-delineated expectations detailed in your job description, but you'll also be aware of the unspoken, implicit expectations of someone in your role. This requires a heightened awareness of how others behave around you, and the effect you have on others during personal interaction. For example, let's say your office allows casual dress instead of suits and ties. That doesn't mean you can come in with torn jeans and a Def Leppard t-shirt. It's implied that you'll meet company expectations, even if they aren't actually written down or codified.

- Finally, role awareness makes you confident, which in turn, makes those around you confident. Those you manage will feel confident, offering suggestions or pointing out problems. Those who manage you will recognize your confidence and feel confident that you can do the job.

"Hell, there are no rules here - we're trying to accomplish something." - *Thomas A. Edison*

WHEN THE LEADER NEEDS TO DELEGATE - SURRENDERING CONTROL

Maintaining confidence in others and being able to delegate responsibility and authority isn't easy to do for many people. Because they feel that only they can do the job correctly, these people are usually overworked and overstressed. They also aren't as productive as they could be because of their perceived workload.

The ability to surrender control in a given situation is characteristic of managers who have high levels of emotional intelligence. They recognize the need to assign responsibilities and then walk away to let the assignee do their job. Even the best managers must sometimes control their natural instinct to micro-manage and oversee every little detail of the work.

When you receive work from those you manage, are you compelled to make changes - to put your stamp of approval on someone else's efforts? Naturally, oversight is an aspect of a manager's work, but there's oversight and then there's over doing it, and if you're over doing it, you're not helping the other members of the team.

You don't have all of the answers and you certainly don't have enough time to handle every task that comes down the pike; you aren't expected to. In fact, your supervisors expect you to know the strengths of your team members and assign the tasks to those best suited to take up the challenge.

Giving up control does not mean sitting idly by as the ship goes down with all hands onboard. As the captain of the ship, you have to know when to take over control and when to give it up. A little guidance now and then is fine, but it's important to the team to know when to back away and give someone else the chance to run things.

Surrendering control allows others to shine and feel the pleasure of success, thus boosting morale. Delegating important tasks and responsibilities facilitates learning within the workplace, enabling other members of the team to develop key skills. Assigning responsibilities also gives you the time and perspective to take in the 'big picture', which is the job of most managers. The fact is, the ability to divvy up the load is one of the most important skills a manager can develop. It requires confidence in your crew and in your judgment of the strengths of others.

You can't do it all. You shouldn't be expected to, nor should you expect those you manage to come to your aid when they've been denied or rebuffed before. Once again, the solid business relationship is one that is built on trust - you trusting others to do the job right and others trusting you to provide the tools necessary to get the job done.

During your workday, there's always plenty to do and surrendering control allows for time to do all the things that need to be done. The skills, attitudes and activities of those who are able to surrender control when the situation calls for it are all associated with the skills described in the emotional intelligence attribute assessment:

- People who are able to surrender control to others are confident in their judgment and in the skills of those around them.
- Managers who possess this attribute are better able to prioritize their work activities, focusing on those activities that require personal attention while delegating less critical tasks to others.
- Supervisors who are able to delegate responsibility and authority take note of the various working styles of team members. Some must have every element in place before moving ahead with an assignment.

Others move forward, gathering necessary elements as they go along. Sometimes, there's no right or wrong way to accomplish a task, as long as it meets expectations - your expectations and the expectations of your managers.

- Good people skills (high EQ) are important for team success. Your ability to surrender control builds the confidence of the other team members and provides them with practical experience in developing their talents for future assignments.

- The delegation of responsibility is not reactive, it's proactive. When you delegate responsibility, you've taken a proactive step that will increase your individual productivity and the productivity of those under your supervision.

The end result of the development of emotional intelligence within the work environment is a people's manager or supervisor - someone who is sensitive to the individual, and not just the task. Managers who shift focus from 'the work' to 'the people' will develop loyalty and respect from subordinates, improve cooperation among team members, increase productivity, and create a work environment that is conducive to the personal growth and happiness of all employees. The work gets done efficiently and people are given credit where and when credit is due.

Your overall goals, as a manager, or supervisor should include:

- Teaching and developing the skills of others, providing both encouragement and guidance.

- Building and enhancing cooperation among the members of your team.

- Accepting responsibility for your work and for the work of those whom you supervise.

- Increasing your understanding of what your tasks are and how they will be accomplished (role awareness) on any given day.

- Learning to delegate responsibility and authority, in effect, surrendering control in certain situations when your time and energy would be put to better use elsewhere.

Whether in the workplace, at home, on the golf course, or while interacting with others in your community, increased emotional intelligence will make your life better, along with the lives of those with whom you live, work and play. The development of these skills, in short, will not only make you a better human being, it will also help others become better human beings - something worthy of serious consideration by anyone.

The ultimate goal of learning about emotional intelligence is to become more aware of our strengths and underdeveloped skills as they relate to our personal and social development. The metaphor we use is becoming a Great Playing Partner. Becoming a great playing partner means that we will be more conscious, more self-aware, more self-controlled, more self-confident, more empathic, and more compassionate. Hopefully, you will not simply read this book, tell yourself it was interesting material and then assume that your job is finished.

On the contrary, we hope this book is only a beginning. For it is our sincere desire that after your first reading, you will read the book again and begin to select two or three of the emotional intelligence competencies, starting with self-awareness and accurate self-assessment, and begin to practice some of the exercises provided throughout the chapters.

Taking the time to grow one's self is a journey, not an event. It requires on-going training and practice, much like a martial arts student starting at white belt and ending up with a black belt. This process of development could have taken the student five years or more. Patience, commitment, self-awareness and determination are all required to meet the mastery standards and the vision the student saw at the very beginning of the journey.

As we discussed earlier in the introduction, emotional intelligence represents only two lines in our human development, namely personal and social skills. There are many more lines of development to choose from for your personal improvement.

The bottom line is this: every human being has the potential to grow beyond where they are today. Most people stagnate in their growth along the way. This doesn't have to be the case. Because we live in such a fast-paced society, who has the time to learn and work on the really important aspects of personal growth? A small percentage take the time. A larger percentage needs to take the time. How about you?

Our families, communities, nation, and the world need each of us to see a greater number of the world's population join in the 'human evolutionary' movement - so that the evolution of humankind continues. If not, what will be the future for our families, communities, the nation, and our world? Will there be more selfishness, more wars, and more hatred? Or, will we experience a greater understanding of ourselves and others, more cooperation among peoples of all countries and more compassion and service to help those in need?

Becoming a great playing partner means that each one of us has the capacity to become more conscious, more self-aware, more self-controlled, more self-confident, more empathic, more joyful, and more compassionate.   *- David Geier*

We want *Score! Power Up Your Game, Business and Life By Harnessing the Power of Emotional Intelligence* to be a catalyst to encourage the readers of this book to start or continue their journey toward becoming a more fully-aware business owner, executive, manager, spouse, parent, golfer, athlete, and citizen of the planet.

The 21st century is an exciting time for every person. We have grown tremendously in our ability to create and advance technology during the last 100 years. We have advanced in technology more in the last 100 years than in the previous 10,000 years. But can we say the same for how we are continuing to develop as conscious human beings?

Many people today are looking for something more in their lives. They are searching for meaning, for being fully alive, and ways to improve and grow, as well as, becoming balanced, functioning humans. One of the biggest problems we have today is the lack of a road map to guide our lives. The developmental road maps are available, but they are not being taught to us. If they were, our emotional intelligence would be rising, not falling, as it has during the last 25 years. The skill sets that emotional intelligence offers is one type of road map that can provide the guidance that children, adolescents and adults need today. But only if we take time to assess ourselves, and apply the exercises to work on ourselves. Then, over time, we will be able to demonstrate the skill as a habit - as a part of our second nature – as part of our emotional intelligence.

In today's fast paced world the trick is to take the time to truly see ourselves and the world around us. To be kind to ourselves and to others, in other words, to be aware. To realize that true happiness and meaningful lives come from being self-aware and being of service to others. Being in the world but not of the world, what a radical concept.   *- John M. Bothwell, Ph.D.*

Appendix

Games Great Playing Partners Can Play

One of the ways to learn how to become a great playing partner is to play games. Not the games people play mind you, but games that provide us an opportunity for learning EQ skills.

The EQ skills that these games promote are: Self-Awareness, Transparency, Adaptability, Achievement Drive, Initiative, Optimism, Teamwork and Collaboration, Conflict Management, Building Bonds, Empathy, Influence, Change Catalyst, and Inspirational leadership.

Self-Awareness:

This skill develops the ability to be aware of our emotions, including our physical and mental states as they arise in the moment.

Transparency:

This skill is the displaying of honesty and integrity.

Adaptability:

This skill is the ability to adapt to changing situations and overcoming obstacles.

Achievement Drive:

This is the drive to improve performance to meet standards of excellence.

Initiative:

This is the readiness to act and seize opportunities. Optimism: Seeing the upside in events.

Teamwork and Collaboration:

This skill promotes cooperation and team building among key executives, managers, supervisors, and employees.

Conflict Management:

The ability to resolve disagreements producing win/win results for all parties involved.

Building Bonds:

This skill cultivates and builds a nest of relationships.

Empathy:

This skill develops a sensitivity for the emotional pain or mental position of another.

Influence:

This skill helps an individual create a range of tactics for persuasion.

Change Catalyst:

This skill promotes the ability to initiate, manage and lead in a new direction.

Inspirational Leadership:

This skill promotes the ability to guide and motivate with a compelling vision.

There are a number of fun golf games that can meet the goal of becoming a great playing partner in business and in golf, here are a few.

THE SCRAMBLE:

This game can be played as a two-person or four-person team. The key to the game is to play the best ball out of the group. Strategic thinking, problem solving, achievement drive and initiative are all needed to play this game well. Played over 18 holes, The Scramble will activate most, if not all, of the EQ competencies listed above.

Teams Playing the Stroke Saver Game:

If time is an issue, this version of The Scramble can be played at a chipping green. The goal is to get the ball up and down in two strokes. The main EQ skill to be practiced is adaptability, teamwork and collaboration and initiative, although many other EQ skills are also being applied. This game can be played in match play or total stroke (medal) formats.

Skins:

This game is designed to enhance one sense of initiative and achievement drive, but as a team concept. Two-person teams are created. A skin is won by the team with the best score, usually par or better. Team members will need to collaborate on who will play the conservative versus more aggressive shot, requiring problem solving and strategic thinking.

Draw Back and Double Draw Back:

This 18-hole game is played on the green. The feature of this two-person game is to draw back the ball one club length if missed on the first putt. This adds to the challenge of the game. This is a total stroke game. In addition, this game enhances intuitive and integrative abilities by reading the putt and using a distance control mental process.

Creative Shot Making:

Making creative shots is one of the important ingredients for playing great golf and becoming a great playing partner. Tour pros Peter Jacobson, Greg Norman and Seve Ballesteros used to play shot making games before the tournament where they would call the shot the other player had to make. This meant hitting high draws, low fades, high slices or shots from under tree branches. The EQ skills this game would develop would be developing others, building bonds, intuition decision making, and inspirational leadership. Points are awarded to the player who best executes the intended shot.

BIBLIOGRAPHY

The Achievement Zone – Shane Murphy, Ph.D.

The Art of Happiness – His Holiness The Dalai Lama and Howard C. Cutler, M.D

Business Golf: The Art of Building Relationships through Golf – Pat Summerall

Birdie, Pars, Bogies: Leadership Lessons from the Links – David Cottrell

Destructive Emotions: How Can We Overcome Them - Daniel Goleman with His Holiness The Dalai Lama

The Double Connexion – Carey Mumford

Essential Spirituality – Roger Walsh

Emotional Intelligence – Daniel Goleman

Emotional Intelligence at Work – Hendrie Weisinger

Go for the Green – Don A. Sanders, Ph.D.

The Golf Profiler Report (Executive Edition) – David G. Geier and Mickey Holmes, CME, CBA

The Golf Magazine Course Management Handbook – Gary Wiren, Ph.D.

Golf By Design – Robert Trent Jones, Jr.

The Heart of a Leader – Ken Blanchard

Integral Psychology – Ken Wilber

Living In Balance – Joel Levey & Michelle Levey

Mind Body Medicine – Daniel Goleman

Playing the Great Game of Golf – Ken Blanchard

Play to Win – Larry Wilson and Hersch Wilson

Principle Centered Leadership – Stephen R. Covey

Primal Leadership – Daniel Goleman, Richard Boyatzis and Annie McKee

The 7 Habits of Highly Effective People – Stephen R. Covey

The Traits of Champions: The Secrets to Championship Performance in Business, Golf, and Life - Andrew Wood and Brian Tracy

Quantum Consciousness – Stephen Wolinsky

Winning in the Game of Life – Tom Gegax

ABOUT THE AUTHORS

JOHN M. BOTHWELL, PH.D. is an international business consultant, author, lecturer, and seminar leader with over 30 years of national and international management and sales expertise. Dr. Bothwell has combined psychology with his many years of real world management and sales consulting experience to help business leaders achieve their goals. Dr. Bothwell was an adjunct professor in the adult education department, on the staffs of Cleveland State University and Terra Community College, prior to moving to Dayton Ohio.

As an aggressive problem solver and recognized industry leader, John Bothwell applies his diverse experience and talents to growing his sales and management consulting firm. John leads his team in implementing strategies and tactics that achieve both company and individual growth for their clients. Working with a variety of companies from Fortune 500 to start-ups, he has developed insights and skills proven to be successful in real-world settings.

John M. Bothwell, Ph.D. has ISO certification in sales and marketing and is a certified senior manufacturing engineer with the Society of Manufacturing Engineers. Other International accreditations include Certified in Marketing and Sales (CMS), Certified Professional Behavior Analyst (CPBA), Certified Professional Values Analyst (CPVA) and Certified Attribute Index Analyst (CAIA).

DAVID G. GEIER is the President and owner of Golf: Inside & Out, an integral golf education company and The Institute of Integral Golf. Prior to entering the golf education field in 1991, David was the owner of Geier & Associates, Inc. a fee-based financial planning firm.

During his fifteen years in the golf business, David has become a leader in the field of golf training and education. His education curriculum is based on the works of American Philosopher Ken Wilber (a leader in integral training, development, and education) and leading teachers in the area of golf such as Harold Swash, Ben Doyle, Tom Tomasello, George Kelnhofer, Geoff Mangum, and Chuck Hogan.

Other influences have come from other cutting-edge thinkers such as Don Beck & Christopher Cowen, Carey Mumford, Larry Miller, George Leonard, Michael Murphy, Joseph Campbell, Roger Walsh, Ken Blanchard, and Sandra Seagal & David Horne.

In 2005, David joined with John Bothwell of The Bothwell Group in the development of a new performance and training program called *Score! Power Up Your Game, Business and Life By Harnessing the Power of Emotional Intelligence* sees golf as a metaphor for self-discovery and development that offers a variety theoretical and practical experiences within the game of golf.

David is the co-author of The Connections Between Business & Golf, Beyond Handicaps and Networking and The Golf Profiler Report – Actual versus Natural Golf Playing Style..

Seminar Topics |

1. Developing the emotionally intelligent manager

Effective leaders have goals and a strategy to achieve them. But sometimes at a visceral level, they become disconnected from their organizations. We will help you evaluate where you are, and how to stay connected with yourself and your organization.

2. The winning edge for success in business and golf

The difference between winning and losing is a slight edge. We will take a look at the next step in your journey-the use of EQ to achieve higher levels of thinking. Your heightened awareness of the concept of EQ, and your on-going, conscious effort to apply the principles that underlie the concept, will be put to use in a number of internal (self-improvement) ways and external (interaction with others) ways. These proficiencies will better equip you for higher-level thinking - outside the box thinking that will be used in virtually every endeavor you undertake.

3. Dynamic leadership and emotional intelligence

There are EQ competencies required for dynamic leadership and growth. We will explore where you are and help you strategize an action plan for growth.

4. Emotional Intelligence and team development

Teamwork is the ability to work together toward a common vision of yourself and the organization. EQ will help you focus individual accomplishments toward organizational objectives.

5. Emotional intelligence, the winning edge in sales

Much has been written about sales and the superior salesperson, but little has changed in recent years in how we select and train our salespeople. Great salespeople are emotionally tough; they possess emotional self-control, and the ability to quickly build relationships. Learn how to develop emotionally intelligent sales people who can and will sell.

6. The art of hiring people who can and will do the job

Numerous studies have demonstrated that EQ is a bigger factor in job success and retention than IQ, and behavioral styles. Learn how to determine the EQ competencies required for success in your job and how to evaluate applicants prior to hiring.

7. The winning edge in customer service.

Increase the EQ of your customer service team and exceed your customer's expectations. Set the stage for success by identifying the core competencies for superior customer service, and identify the skills necessary to consistently deliver on the promises of great customer service to both internal and external customers.

8. The art of consistently delivering effective patient services.

The emotionally intelligent physician and nurse live the values of excellence, integrity, and service to create patient-centered quality care. We can help you develop an environment of team work, and reduce the stress of delivering quality patient care.

9. Reduce medical malpractice through the use of emotional intelligence and advanced communication skills.

Developing protocols for a comfortable and professional relationship with your patients requires high emotional intelligence and advanced communication skills. Let's face it, medical malpractice begins with the receptionist and extends to the doctors' interactions with their patients. Patients who feel well cared for and have an emotional connection, and comfortable relationship with their physicians rarely sue, even when there may be a less than satisfactory outcome to patient care. Learn how to evaluate the EQ of your practice and develop a protocol for improved patient relationships.

10. How to SCORE in the Boardroom and the Bedroom.

We will explore how to take the leadership skills important for success in the boardroom and develop them for balance, and success in your personal life as well. One of the keys to winning in life is balance. Use EQ to insure that balance and win in life.

SEMINARS ARE AVAILABLE in half-day, full-day, and multi-session formats. EQ assessments and feedback are available for all seminars. Dr. Bothwell is also available as a keynote speaker, www.SCOREEQ.com.

| FREE OFFER |

EQ thought of the week, emailed weekly. *Retail value $39.00 per year.*

For more details, visit **WWW.SCOREEQ.COM**.

Printed in the USA
CPSIA information can be obtained
at www.ICGtesting.com
JSHW082204140824
68134JS00014B/420